# Redemptive
# Missiology
# In Pneumatic
# Context

# Endorsements

I have heard it said, if you speak from your mind, you reach another mind. If you speak from your heart, you reach another heart. This book speaks from the heart, and will touch your heart. It touched mine.

**Ken Groen**
*Regional Superintendent, Open Bible Churches, (ret.),
Des Moines, Iowa*

When I am asked to review a literary work of this type, the first things I want to know are: (1) Does he really believe this? (2) Does he practice it? (3) How much passion does he have for his exposition? All three of these questions were met positively by Joe Girdler in the work at hand. I believe Redemptive Missiology is something that needs to be repeated over and over again, especially by people who really believe in it and are passionate about the subject. Throughout the years I have known Joe and Renee, I have seen this on display in every sense of the word. I believe the content of his work is biblical, on-target, and lived in their daily lives.

**L. John Bueno**
*Missionary, El Salvador, Former Executive Director of
World Missions, Assemblies of God (ret.)*

One of my favorite memories in life is a trip to Ecuador I made with Pastor Joe. I still love telling the rat story. Pastor Joe is more than qualified to write about missions; he lived it as a pastor as he led the way in the KY Network in missions giving. He has lived it as a man, gone on several trips, and now has family giving time to missions. He has lived it as a superintendent, making missions the priority for our network. He served as an example to Cathy and me when we pastored in Kentucky and now serves as a support to us as we serve overseas. I highly recommend reading and applying his wisdom in missions.

**Kevin Stone**
*Area Director Arab World*

When it comes to missiology, Dr. Joseph Girdler thoroughly knows the subject. He leads and teaches from a world of hands-on experience. From District Mission director, while he and Renee pastored a thriving mission-minded congregation, to superintendent of the Kentucky Ministry Network, Joe leads with passion and compassion for missions and missionaries. His concise work will provide theological answers to the questions of why and practical applications for pastors, churches, and individuals looking for ways to put their missiology into practice.

**Bill McDonald**
*Founder, Unsion International Television Network, Ecuador*

Dr. Joseph S. Girdler is, and always will be, "Pastor Joe" to my wife and me. As friends and colleagues for more than 25 years, several things have always been clear about him: he loves his family, he is deeply in love with and committed to Jesus, and he is passionate about global missions. All these things come through clearly in this book. I highly recommend that you take the time to read this book. It is filled with spiritual insights, touching and relevant stories, and practical helps about how we can reach and serve the world on God's global mission. As a strategic leader with Assemblies of God World Missions in one of the least reached areas in the world, I can honestly say that the students who initially heard these lectures were blessed to be encouraged to participate in the harvest by Dr. Girdler's lectures. Reading this book gives you the same sense of Spirit-driven urgency and exhortation—as well as the pastoral heart—that these students had when they listened to them. May we see more churches sending and more workers in the harvest—doing so in the power of the Holy Spirit—as a result of this book.

**Edward and Kimberly Nye**
*Area Directors, Central Eurasia*

My wife, Charlotte, and I were in the first months of our itineration in preparation to serve in Argentina. We had just concluded a youth missions service at our home church in Lexington, KY, and the youth pastor handed me a note that he had found in the offering plate. It was from a dear friend, a college student. The note, dated March 16, 1986, said, "My offering to you today is my life, with Renee to the service of God wherever he may lead. - Joe" Joe's heart for evangelism and missions began very early in his walk with the Lord and shines brightly in this volume, Redemptive Missiology in Pneumatic Context. You will weep as you read of the painful experiences that he faced as a child and a young man, but then as you follow his journey, Joe's Spirit-led compassion will inspire you to cry out, "Father, use me in a greater way to reach hurting, lost people from my doorstep to the ends of the earth!"

**Martin Jacobson**
*Missionary 30+ years, Director,*
*Patagonia Bible Institute, (ret.) Argentina*

It was a great honor to have Dr. Joseph Girdler present the following mission lectures to the students, faculty, and staff at Continental Theological Seminary during our 2018 Missions Convention. This book offers a passionate plea for a Spirit-empowered approach to missions. Dr. Girdler brings his many years of experience in missions, denominational leadership, and pastoral ministry to bear in laying out the privilege and responsibility of what he calls "being a Great Commission Christian." The book provides an effective theological and biblical rationale for commitment to missional praxis at both the personal and ecclesial levels of Christian life. We were blessed by these lectures and I trust you will be as well.

**David Trementozzi**
*PhD, Vice President, Academics,*
*Continental Theological Seminary*

Redemptive Missiology is a reflection of Dr. Joe Girdler's passion for missions and is an excellent guide and motivation for how to build that similar passion in your church team. You will find the reasoning of Jesus's direction to the Church and a straightforward approach to missions success that will make you a leader as well.

**David Girdler**
*Mechanical Engineer (ret.) and former Vice President of Operations of three international chemical and pharmaceutical organizations*

"Go into all the world and make disciples." This is not the great suggestion but the Great Co-Mission; us working together with God to make His Good News known to all people in all places. It would seem, however, that sometimes we forget and need to remind ourselves. Dr. Joseph S. Girdler has done a great service in these pages to bring us back once again to why we are here and what it truly means to be a disciple of Jesus the Christ. Missions. The call of Jesus is "follow me," and He is always going. We must go, too. Thank you, Dr. Girdler, for resounding that clear, unmistakable, and unrelenting toll for all who have ears to hear!

**Steve Turley**
*Global Missionary, Croatia, Belgium, Europe*

Dr. Girdler's book Redemptive Missiology in Pneumatic Context is a passionate and personal read from the understanding of a pastor and leader in the Assemblies of God regarding the work of the Holy Spirit in missions. He outlines a framework of redemptive contextualization, missional pneumatology, financial contextualization, and cultural contextualization. The book is concise and to the point, while incorporating his own unique style of illustrations.

**Dr. Greg Mundis**
*Springfield, Missouri, Executive Director - Assemblies of God World Missions*

This book is not for those who protect the status quo in their spiritual walk and ministry. As I read chapter one, "Why Is Missions Important?" I found myself weeping. To see God's purpose for the Church and the individual believer compared to the actual spiritual condition of the Church and its members brought tears that I could scarcely control. As I continued reading, I found myself wishing that this book could be required reading by every pastor and every church member who truly desires to live and work according to God's will.

I have known the author, Joe Girdler, for most of his Christian walk. During this time we have built a very close relationship. So close, in fact, that I call him "Son" and he calls me "Dad." I have watched him grow in both his walk with the Lord and God's blessings upon his ministry. What he writes here is not theory, but experience directed by the Holy Spirit. I encourage you to read this book with an open heart and mind, allowing God to guide you to those areas where you need special personal attention. Our one responsibility while we walk on this earth is to reach the lost for Christ! Nothing else matters!

***Paul Brannan***

*Branson West, Missouri, Assemblies of God Missionary for 50+ years (ret.), former Executive Leadership Committee (ELC), Assemblies of God World Missions, Asst. Superintendent/Missions Dir., Kentucky Ministry Network, Assemblies of God (ret.)*

# Redemptive Missiology In Pneumatic Context

*Practical Missions Led by the Holy Spirit*

## Joseph S. Girdler, D.Min

*Meadow Stream*
PUBLISHING

# Redemptive
# Missiology
# In Pneumatic
# Context
© 2019 by Joseph S. Girdler

Published in Crestwood, Kentucky by **Meadow Stream Publishing.**

ISBN 978-1-7337952-2-7 paperback
ISBN 978-1-7337952-3-4 eBook

*Meadow Stream*
PUBLISHING

# Dedication

*This book is dedicated to my children, Steven and Rachel. Traveling with them both on missions trips across the world as they were growing up remain as some of my greatest memories of dad-hood. There is no greater honor I have ever been given than that of being their dad. I have amazing joy of the recollections, from watching my son hold a chimpanzee in the edge of the Amazon forest after a long day of ministry, passing out flyers, and personally inviting Amazonia residents to the outreach service upcoming, to seeing my daughter a few years later light up with life in the lobby of a Quito hotel as she personally met and welcomed a beautiful six-year-old Ecuadorian child into our family's world as we began monthly support for Jessenia to attend a Christian school.*

*With their lovely and godly mother, Renee (my college girlfriend), they are God's gifts to me. I could not be more proud of the adults they've become. How they both live life to its fullest, offer the epitome of servanthood, laugh, love, and strive to give more of themselves every day for the betterment of others; they have always challenged me.*

*(Steven and Rachel, you both are world-changers. You've already changed mine. I love you more than you'll ever know, and I love being your dad.)*

# Table of Contents

# Acknowledgements

Let me first say, I am deeply grateful for Renee, my life partner, who accompanied me to Brussels for these lectures, and who also ministered while there. And, I am deeply appreciative to my editor, Catherine McGee, and to indisputable professionals, Brad and Hilton Rahme of Uberwriters (www.uberwriters.com) for their technical and publishing support.

This book is about the mission of man for the work of God. I respectfully offer my utmost appreciation to those few individuals who have taught me most about the missional journey. So many names come to mind who have given extra effort to me in missions as I ponder the past three or four decades in ministry. I think of my pastor, Ken (and Nadine) Groen, at a church in Lexington, Kentucky, when I was in college. It was there I first saw a pastor lead missionally, challenge a congregation to reach miracle-level giving achievements, and hear firsthand accounts from global workers around the world giving me a burden and a challenge to reach the lost with the life-giving gospel of Christ.

Acknowledgements

I'm grateful for the opportunities I've been given to meet and know personally world missions denominational leaders like the late Loren Triplett, John and Lois Bueno, Greg and Sandie Mundis, and so many others who have become personal friends and encouraged me with their global heartbeat.

Without Paul (and Betty) Brannan, with a fifty-plus-year career in missions, speaking repeatedly into my life through the years, offering me—in any way I could ever use it—his detailed writings and work from many years of missions leadership and leadership training, and ultimately his becoming a beloved father figure to me personally, I would not know what I've come to learn or have the same heartbeat and passions for the lost to which I've come to understand and have shared with countless thousands through the years.

To friends Steve and Deanne Turley, amazing global workers, who actually hosted my first travel and ministry visit to Brussels in 2005, thank you for challenging me as a young pastor desiring to build a missions-hearted church, yet struggling with the realities of small-church budgets and challenged faith, with the "you can't afford not to give..." You continue to inspire.

With over twenty missions travels to our now beloved Ecuador, I give deep respect to dear friends and missionaries Bill and Connie McDonald, whose heart for the peoples of Latin America and visionary motivations have left an indelible mark upon my life and that of my family. I've traveled that great nation with Bill numerous times from Quito to Guayaquil, from Cuenca to Sucua, and numerous villages in between. Our ministry together has included medical outreaches, ministering at preaching points, leading community outreaches to countless teenagers through the years, and endeavoring to impact society with Christian-worldview television through the Unsion television network family. Through it all, his passions and commitments to the remarkable people of Ecuador have given me a firsthand account of Jesus's stunning command when he told the Pharisees, "'Love the Lord your God with all your heart and with all your soul and with all your mind.' This is the first and greatest commandment. And the second is like it: 'Love your neighbor as yourself'" (Matt. 22:37–40, NIV).

I watched my own father-in-law through the years, the late Rev. Lorie Vannucci, who pastored a small and rural Eastern Kentucky congregation he'd planted forty-five years prior to his passing, always make it a priority to bless the missionary speaker that would make the extra effort and drive to come to his church. Rarely did they walk away with less than a $1,000 offering from that small church, and more times than one could count, they'd return with a new suit as well.

Acknowledgements

Finally, I want to thank the local church youth and young adult pastors at the time that I had given my life wholeheartedly to the Lord during my college years, and who—upon my own university graduation—gave me the occasion of joining them on my first missions trip in 1984 to Mexico City, which altered my entire trajectory for life and ministry: thirty-plus-year global workers to Argentina, Martin and Charlotte Jacobson. The lessons in humility I learned by watching their lives and the opportunities on three different occasions from 1989 to 2014 to minister, witness, and sense firsthand the yearning and thirsts for the things of God through the lens of what has been known as a global-awakening Argentine revival, has had by far more of an impact on my life than anything I could have ever brought to those to whom the Lord allowed me to minister on those occasions.

These friends have remarkably impacted my life. They are each genuine leaders and have helped mold this heart for missions. Now, let's mold the next generation until He comes.

# Introduction

Missions, next to family, remains my passion. I have vivid memories of seeing the wall-length banners hanging in the church I attended while at university, announcing the $100,000 missions-giving goals for the year ahead. I had never seen anything of that nature before. I certainly had never been to a church where global missions had been given such priority and emphasis. Only ten years later, I found myself pastoring a local church nearby. It was my highest of honors. I hope I made a difference.

Serving as a denominational leader, a privileged mantle, allowed me to be more involved in missions than ever before. Leading others to a personal relationship with Jesus—beyond exceptional. Guiding Christ followers to a healthier understanding of their Savior's mandate (Go Ye Therefore) in the discipleship journey—a thrill. Seeing others who were yet to know Him or know of His Word, His promises, find His truly amazing grace—nothing like it. That season in college, I was learning about God, what He had said, what He was like, and what He was saying to me then; *theology*, if you will. In the journey, I recognized *mission* (at least in this general sense) was what I was doing about it. Mission became all about us (or me) and our involvement in God's beckoning to share in the amazing redemptive story of the Cross.

A book of this nature must have at its core a mission-centered theology of the Cross. Everything for a genuine follower of Christ begins and ends from the Cross. It is mission theology within itself. God's mission was to redeem all humankind and renew and restore through the inescapable death and subsequently miraculous burial and resurrection of Jesus Christ.

These missional lectures you are about to experience were from a series of presentations I was honored to offer by way of the invitation from Seminary President Dr. Joseph Dimitrov and Seminary Dean Dr. David Trementozzi at Continental Theological Seminary, Brussels, Belgium, November 26–29, 2018. I offer my deepest respects to these esteemed colleagues and indubitable appreciation for their friendships and encouragements in offering Renee and me the opportunity to speak into the lives of some remarkable next-generation leaders of today's global church. As you read these lectures and spend time with the topics and insights offered, keep in mind I've purposefully attempted to maintain the original context intact (with some added expansions needed for book contextualization and a reader's considerations) from actual transcriptions of the events, allowing the reader to envision themselves as a part of the audience when the presentations were given.

Many leaders have spoken into my own life over the years. I certainly want to bring credit to any original source(s), provided I know where the source would have originated. As would be with any presenter, so many things that have become second nature to my reflections were imparted to me throughout the course of my own journey. I am deeply grateful to all who would have stirred conversation through the years for every point and insight and each concept or consideration that has become a part of these presentations. To you: Thank you for allowing me into your world—allowing me your thoughts and ideas—that we together might make an impact for the Kingdom. My heart is that we make more than an impact. May we make a difference.

*Pastor Joe*

# Foreword

If we remove the pneumatic force from Christian missions, the church will be in the world but also of the world. Then what was divinely assigned will become humanly performed. It is the Holy Spirit that leads the church to minister to the world and yet protects the church from the world. In this book Dr. Girdler makes it clear that only in the pneumatic context we could correctly understand Christ's mandate to the church for missions. It addresses the missional nature of the church, the true purpose of mission finances, and the understanding of culture that aims at the proclamation of the gospel. A Spirit-driven mission would not miss any of these three!

**Joseph Dimitrov**
*PhD, President, Continental Theological Seminary,*
*Brussels, Belgium*

Redemptive Contextualization: Redemptive
Missiology in Pneumatic Context
Why Is Missions Important?

Thank you so much. We are deeply, humbly honored to be here.

> *"Christian pneumatology refers to a specific theological discipline that concentrates on the analysis and study of the Holy Spirit."*

Christian pneumatology refers to a specific theological discipline that concentrates on the analysis and study of the Holy Spirit. The expression is principally derived from the Greek word *pneuma* (πνεῦμα), designating "breath" or "spirit."

We are here for one reason. I recently heard friend and missional colleague Dr. Beth Grant proclaim, "Missions is not a program. It is the heartbeat of God." I, too, fully embrace the same. There is but one name that matters. And His name is Jesus. He is the author and finisher of my faith. He's the one who saved me, delivered me, set me free… gave me everything that I have in my life. My today. My tomorrow. He is the reason we live and breathe and have our very being. His name is Jesus.

Prayer—You are such a good, good God; A good father. Give us ears to hear what you might speak to your church in the majestic and mighty name of Jesus. Amen.

It is an honor to be with you today. Thank you, and, please call me "Joe."

I brought gifts for:
The chairman of your missions committee, Ms. Catherine.
Missionaries who helped my wife and me, Deanne and Steve Turley.
Dr. David Trementozzi, a blessing to CTS and a friend to our family.
My wife and I are a team. We were college students when we met. We do everything together. So representatively, this gift is for Dr. Dimitrov's wife, Yvette. You know him as professor or president. But, you only know half of him. She's his better half. ☺

And, of course, last but not of least these personal gifts are for him, our esteemed seminary president, Dr. Joseph Dimitrov.

Further, and with the help of a number of friends and churches across Kentucky, the additional monetary gift offered is for this beautiful seminary, Continental Theological Seminary, Brussels, Belgium.

Let us begin.

Redemptive Contextualization: Redemptive Missiology in Pneumatic Context. Why Is Missions Important? Wow. Ha ha ha. So, I defined that with "Why is Missions Important?"

The next slide is my inspiration—a photo of my family. I am nothing without them: my wife, my daughter, and my son and daughter-in-law.

I grew up the son of humble beginnings. The youngest of four, to which my siblings would say I was spoiled, we each were challenged with our early home-life. We dealt with those early year trials uniquely and differently, almost as if they were a selected test for life ahead, and respectively found our ways with meaning, achievement, and reconciled peace. I wholeheartedly gave my life to Christ while a student in college. An apartment roommate was murdered shortly after I had moved out of the flat. That actually impacted me more than most knew. I didn't even know the roommate all that well, but it was during those years I was learning to hear the voice of God. It had been just weeks prior to his passing that I sensed a distinct spiritual discernment to move and find other living arrangements.

During those years, I had relationships that were un-healthy. My focus on academics was shallow, at best. And though fully trusting a God of the universe, I desperately needed an intimately personal relation-ship with God.

> *"We dealt with those early year trials uniquely and differently, almost as if they were a selected test for life ahead."*

Mustering the forthwithal to attend a church by myself at the invitation of a friend, I sat in the very back of the building, in the last pew of the row on the end, right next to a side door. It was a church of about a 750 to 1,000. That particular day, for the first time in my life, I tangibly sensed the presence of God. I continued to attend that church alone and in time found a new spot in the auditorium to the far left from my initial seat. Now more center-isled and a few pews into the sanctuary, I'd typically sit—still solitary—at the end of one of the long blue pews. Some weeks later, I looked ahead of me during the time of music, singing, and praise and worship. About six rows ahead—her back was to me—I saw the most beautiful gazelle I had ever seen in my life. (Laughter.) So...I continued going to church. (Laughter, again.) When I gathered enough faith to ask her to dinner, she told me on the first night, "I will not marry a man not baptized in the Holy Spirit." Wow, that was direct, and, on a first date, nonetheless. So, I came back to church (laughter, again) ...and went to an altar. The rest is history.

*I sat in the very back of the building, in the last pew of the row on the end, right next to a side door.*

We do what we do because of pneumatological Christology: the Holy Spirit upon the life and ministry of Jesus...and those called by His name. We are called to Christ-likeness that we might walk in the newness of life—a disciple, a follower, a believer in the Great Redeemer who lives! We do what we do because of pneumatological missiology. Truly your pneumatology develops your theology. Jesus was always in the Spirit. The Spirit was evident in every part of His life. And, so, it should be ours as well.

*"About six rows ahead—her back was to me—I saw the most beautiful gazelle I had ever seen in my life."*

I think of missionary friends who exemplify this very walk, the late Jacque and Johanna Vernaud from Kinshasa, Congo, the founding pastors of the great 12,000-member LaBorne Church. (Johanna passed and was buried just outside Kinshasa this past August 2018.) As with the Vernauds, you and I can only offer the redeeming power of

Christ to those who see it lived out in our own lives. It's not how much you know. As we've heard it said before, it's all about "who" you know.

The calling in Ephesians is for the Church to fulfill her role in the mission of God—for the Church to participate in the *missio Dei*. God's mission flows as a current:

- from God the Father,
- to Jesus Christ the Son,
- to the Holy Spirit who empowers the church to carry on the mission to the world (Eph. 1:10).

Think of the calling of Paul in Ephesus. I've been there—the great cathedral of learning, that great amphitheater of Paul's trouble. It was there the world was changed. The calling in the book of Ephesians is for the church to fulfill the mission of God, for the church to participate in *missio Dei*.

I recognize you've had powerful evangelists and preachers through the years minister here in Brussels. And I am a preacher. I love to preach. I can only bring you what I feel

> *"My prayer is that missions will no longer be a program but the call and heart of God."*

God has told me to bring, so it will be a little of preaching and a little of lecture. But, my prayer is that when we're done you will have received a little more of the gospel, that missions will no longer be a program but the call and heart of God, and that this will not be a missions convention but a way of life.

Let's address, momentarily, brokenness.

> *"In him we have redemption through his blood, the forgiveness of our trespasses, according to the riches of his grace, which he lavished upon us..."* Ephesians 1:7–8 (ESV)

> *"In him you also, when you heard the word of truth, the gospel of your salvation, and believed in him, were sealed with the promised Holy Spirit, who is the guarantee of our inheritance until we acquire possession of it..."* Ephesians 1:13–14 (ESV)

> *"When Christ calls a man, he bids him come and die."* Dietrich Bonhoeffer

But the world today wants it easy..."I've wanted it easy," most say. "I just wanted to be happy." I've pondered these thoughts for years and heard or read numerous authors allude to the same. Theologians, church leaders, pastors: Is there any concern at all about the Jerusalem that is in our own hearts? Are there any concerned about a sweeping coldness widespread across the land? Or, that God's spiritual Jerusalem, the Church, is now married to the world? Overall, today's Church is blind to lukewarm-ness, blind to the mixture of the world that is creeping in.

Bonhoeffer wrote *The Cost of Discipleship* in 1937. This rich volume was a call to more faithful and radical obedience to Christ and... he wrote it as a severe rebuke of comfortable Christianity:

*"Cheap grace is preaching forgiveness without requiring repentance, baptism without church discipline, Communion without confession... Cheap grace is grace without discipleship, grace without the cross, grace without Jesus Christ, living and incarnate."*

> *"Overall, today's Church is blind to lukewarm-ness, blind to the mixture of the world that is creeping in."*

Some years ago I was preaching and doing ministry in Great Britain/England. I had the privilege to sit with an extended and now distant family member of Smith Wigglesworth. Wigglesworth said,

*"The reason the world is not seeing Jesus is that Christian people are not filled with Jesus. They are satisfied with attending meetings weekly, reading the Bible occasionally, and praying sometimes. It is an awful thing for me to see people who profess to be Christians lifeless, powerless, and in the place where their lives are so parallel to unbelievers' lives that it is difficult to tell which place they are in, whether the flesh*

*or the Spirit."*

The Assistant General Superintendent of San Antonio, TX, Alton Garrison said, "The average attendance in 2017 for US churchgoers is now 1.9 times per month." (AG USA November 6, 2018) Compare this to nearly 4 times per month only 15 years ago and what would have been likely 7 to 8 times per month 40 years ago.

There is going to be no renewal, nor Church awakening, until we are willing to let Him break us. We often sing about being broken. God uses broken things. Jesus took the bread and broke it. The alabaster box was broken. Jesus said, "This is my body which was broken for you."

> *"God uses broken things."*

Second Chronicles 7:14 is the clarion call that:

> *"If my people, who are called by my name, will humble themselves, and pray and seek my face..."*
> 2 Chronicles 7:14 (ESV)

There is no getting around that step—redemptive missiology in pneumatic context. There is no getting around the "people called by my name," humbling themselves to pray and seek His face...and if we will do that...and if we will...

> *"...and turn from their wicked ways, then I will*

> *hear from heaven and will forgive their sin and will heal their land."* 2 Chronicles 7:14 (ESV)

Some of us need our own homes healed. We need our families healed. We need our children healed, our marriages healed, or our pasts healed. Oh, but I met the Healer. I met the Redeemer. I met the One and True God who changes lives. Missions is not a program. Missions is the heartbeat of God. I first heard it most recently worded in terms like that listening to Dr. Beth Grant (Executive Director, Project Rescue) speak at a leadership event in San Antonio, Texas. Everybody you know, meet, and see needs to know my Jesus. They need healing. He carries it in His wings. And He surrounds you.

> *"There is no getting around the 'people called by my name,' humbling themselves to pray and seek His face."*

Are God's leaders willing to say to God, "I am not what I was. I am not where I am supposed to be. God, I don't have Your heart or Your burden?" It will begin there: humbly denying self, dying to self, asking God for His burdens to be yours.

> *"Missiology begins with asking God to allow you to see with His eyes, His lens, and His view."*

Missiology begins with asking

10

God to allow you to see with His eyes, His lens, and His view—to see people as He sees people. When you see me, you judge me based on what you see, but you do not know what's inside of me—where I've come from, what I've dealt with. You know one for what you see. You do not know what one cries for, what burdens one. What you do not see is that we are all the same, all broken without Jesus. All of us need the recognition of our brokenness and the promises and relationship, healing and peace from the Redeeming God. You do not know what you do not ask. You do not know a God that you do not spend time with. But when you spend time with Him, you do not know them from their outer shell—you know "them" (others you meet and interact with) from that inner place, the deeper recesses of their heart and soul. It changes what you think about individuals, and it changes the compassion in your heart for them.

Let's address, momentarily, humility and the life of those who hunger to walk in this powerful virtue, coupled with certain and inevitable trials the world brings to our doorsteps. James 4:7–10 says,

> *"Submit yourselves therefore to God. Resist the devil, and he will flee from you. 8 Draw near to God, and he will draw near to you. Cleanse your hands, you sinners, and purify your hearts, you double-minded. 9 Be wretched and mourn and weep. Let your laughter be turned to mourning and your joy to gloom. 10 Humble yourselves*

*before the Lord, and he will exalt you."*

James 4:7–10 (ESV)

The Scripture bears out five steps regarding humility and seeing that rich virtue genuinely revealed in your life.

1. Submit yourself to God (4:7a)
2. Resist Satan's attacks and temptations (4:7b)
3. Take the first step nearer to God (4:8a)
4. Admit your evil, unholy, and sinful nature (4:8b)
5. Get serious about the Kingdom (4:9)

Further, there are four dangerous steps in the believer's relationship with the world. You can find those listed through passages as these:

1. Becoming entangled in a friendship with the world (James 4:4)
2. Finding one actually loving the world and the things of the world (1 John 2:15–17)
3. Ultimately conforming to the world and her low mores and sinful standards (Rom. 12:1–2)
4. Finding one then, judged with the world and those of the world (1 Cor. 11:32)

To be missions-minded we must recognize some things about the world. We must come humbly. It begins with our own breaking and our humility before the Father. But, we need to understand some things about the world.

Friendship, love, conformity, and being judged with the world—these are things that will keep us from carrying the touch of God and the mantle of His presence.

Keep in mind our context is pneumatic missiology—the Spirit of God living within us which changes our view of the world. Many of us know this passage: "Present your bodies a living sacrifice..." (Rom. 12:1–2, ESV). It has to do with our understanding of how we view the world. You can't direct someone to accept Jesus unless they meet Jesus.

> *"Friendship, love, conformity, and being judged with the world— these are things that will keep us from carrying the touch of God and the mantle of His presence."*

The church cannot look like the world; we cannot live like the world; we cannot be conformed to the world. But instead we should present a holy sacrifice—acceptable— which the Bible says is our reasonable service. If we do not, we will be judged with the world.

First Corinthians 11 speaks to the context of if we will judge ourselves and have faith in the redemptive work of Christ on the Cross, we will then not go without His promises. And, your countenance will not be conformed to the world, ...and your love of the father will not be of the world, ...and your friendship to Christ will not be as the world. Rather, it will be like Jesus when He sat in the Mount of Olives and overlooked the great walled city of Jerusalem. The Bible said as He prayed, looking at the world, and He wept.

Prayer: O God, Let us weep again. May the joy of our salvation which overflows in our abundant praise to you, O God put a burden in our hearts, a weeping and a mourning in our spirits for those who don't know Him, who have not been healed, and who do not know. And, Lord, as Isaiah said, Woe is me. I am undone. Here am I. Send me, O God.

How many of you here today would say in your heart, "O God, send me. O God, break me. O God, give me eyes that I might see. Redeem me that I might be made whole and able to fulfill your mandate to 'Go ye therefore'"? What keeps me from it?

Redemptive missiology confesses three pronounced adversaries:

1. The world in which we live—the earthly realm (the habitation of spiritual adultery) (Rom. 7:4; 2 Cor. 11:2).
2. Our own flesh—(that sensual place of temptations directed at and tugging on every man and woman) lusts = desires (Rom. 8:3–7; Gal. 5:16–18, 5:24).
3. Satan—the Devil, the accuser, the tempter, and his dominions (the adversary himself). And, remember,

when pride sets in the devil takes over (Zech. 3:1–2; John 8:44, 10:10; 1 Cor. 7:5; James 4:7).

James 3:15 says the wisdom of the world is different than God. God's wisdom is not worldly, not earthly. Spiritual adultery is how the world functions. And, not one temptation you've experienced did Christ not also.

> *"Spiritual adultery is how the world functions."*

But, grace. Grace is for the lowly, not the lofty. And, for the believer, remember this: God cannot help the Christian who is proud.

There are some today whose chief concern is to be a specialist. Leonard Ravenhill spoke of those that God had called to specialize in the spiritual decline of the nation and in the church. God has always had individuals, called men and women of faith and power, whose primary concerns have been the decline of society's spiritual health.

For students here at CTS (Brussels, Belgium), there are many places you could go to seminary, but God directed you here. If you are in the center of His will for your lives, I would say to you, "Don't sell out too cheaply." Realize God's hand is upon you to change the world around you.

> *"Don't sell out too cheaply."*

Elijah, Jeremiah, Malachi, and other apostolic and prophetic missional leaders appeared at critical moments in history to reprove, rebuke, and exhort. You are here, in the name of Christ—God—and for righteousness to do the same.

God is raising up a generation that will not be as the norm, will not be as the world, but will stand with a standard above, living by a challenged call. And when you walk in a room, humbly, filled with God's presence, with the eyes of the Father, and a tear—if not in your eyes, at the least in your hearts—God will direct you to where His Spirit is already working and you will be world-changers for the gospel. Such a man—then and now—is likely to be drastic, radical, possibly at times violent to the enemy and his schemes. And, the curious crowds who gather to watch will brand him or her as extreme, fanatical, and negatively irrelevant.

> *"God is raising up a generation that will not be as the norm, will not be as the world, but will stand with a standard above, living by a challenged call."*

Leaders of this nature for today's Church will not be unlike those of the Bible. They will shock some, frighten others, and alienate not a few, but will know of Whom they are called and to what they are called to do.

16

John the Baptist was peculiar, eccentric, odd, strange—but he was pronounced, distinct, marked, and great in his own calling! He challenged the people. He cried, "Repent!"

Leonard Ravenhill said, *"John the Baptist was strange. He was strange in his doctrine, strange in his diet, and strange in the way he dressed. But, he was also great. He was great in his fidelity, great in his submission to the Spirit, and great in his statements of the son of God, Jesus Christ."*

He was a voice. Most preachers are only echoes of someone they've heard, someone they've read, someone they desire to be like or sound like. But to reach the lost we need a Voice. We need world-changers. We need those called to not sell out too cheaply. We need those called to go the way of the untrodden path, where others would dare not go and would question the way, the why, or the how of getting there. We need those called to take the first steps in faith, believing and knowing that God will then illuminate the way for the next.

*"They will shock some, frighten others, and alienate not a few, but will know of Whom they are called and to what they are called to do."*

*"It takes broken men, to break men,"* Ravenhill preached. *"This generation of preachers is responsible for this generation of sinners. Sin today is both glamorized and popularized, by movies, television, radio, advertising, magazines, and books. But, we need (in these confusing days) new men; men with a new message. John cried, Repent."*

We need voices not worried if they gain the accolades but willing to bring a new message of life for the sake of the gospel. We need men and women with a new message. John cried, "Repent!" Who takes the challenge? To love people for who they are. To not judge them for their lives, but to draw them to the Cross, to a place of understanding that there is a redeeming God who will heal and change their lives from today—the present and now moments of life—through all of eternity.

> *"We need voices not worried if they gain the accolades but willing to bring a new message of life for the sake of the gospel."*

Let's take a moment to talk about His presence and our dwelling in Him. Redemption comes through the power of the Holy Spirit working in lives! It's all about His Presence...

Exodus 34:29 spoke of Moses, "His face glowed from being in the presence of God" (TLB). In other words, His presence rubs off on you. Redemptive missiology—God's Presence rubs off on you. And, when you are around others who do not have it, His presence rubs off on them.

With a friend, you do things together, and in your heart of hearts you are desperate to show him Jesus. You want to find a way to tell him all the things wrong in his life, but the love of God constrains you to simply love him. It rubs off—the friend leaves and sits down privately with his wife, for instance, and he will say, I don't know what it is about him or about her. It's just something different. I want what they've got. Then, before you know it, the friend starts calling you because the Holy Spirit is attractive. It draws people. When you love me for who I am—not judging me for my wrong, just showing me Jesus— I want to know... that...Jesus. Not the one most churches give me, but the one you show me because He's a good, good Father.

> "It's all about His Presence."

Think of these three things.

1. You can only talk compellingly or convincingly, I once heard, about the God you know! -The one you've spent time with. Any other God belongs in a theology book, and you'll have a hard time promoting Him.

2. When Moses came down the mountain, his face glowed. He'd been in God's presence. And, when you've been there IT SHOWS. When I pastored years earlier in life, I

once preached a several week series on the presence of
God upon Moses's life. When His presence is upon you,

It shows:
in the way you look...
in the way you walk...
in the way you spend
your money...

> *"When His presence is
> upon you, it shows in
> the way you look...
> in the way you walk...
> in the way you spend."*

> *"For us,
> missions is not a program, it is the heart of
> God."* Beth Grant, Project Rescue.

...and in the way you respond to hurting people. It
rubs off. How you walk with the broken is more
important than how you sit with the great, someone
said.

3. Most of us are as close to God as we want to be. James
   4:8 says, "Draw near to God, and he will draw near to
   you."

How could you possibly be the same when you've been
with Him? How could you possibly not love the lost when
you've been with Him? He went to a cross and gave His life
that I might have life.

I was 20 years old when I sat in the back of that church

and for the first time in my life sensed His presence. Not too long thereafter, with having lost a roommate and recognizing my life was in shambles, I knew I needed the Lord. My family loved me...but when I went to my university only about 70 miles from my home, my father took me and dropped me off my first day—gave me a hug and told me he loved

> "I was 20 years old when I sat in the back of that church and for the first time in my life sensed His presence."

me. He did love me. I never questioned that. Still, he never returned for the next four years. Certainly, those were the days before modern technology, the days before cell phones or easy access transportation routes. One can deliberate numerous reasons why elderly parents could not easily get away to visit their son. On occasions I would visit them by returning to my home, yet from that point in life, I felt I was on my own.

But that day, in that church, I met a friend closer than a brother and he changed my life. Most of us are as close to God as we want to be but...He transforms everything He touches. I knew about God. I talked about God. I

> "He didn't say to visit or drop by. He said dwell."

lived a relatively clean life, purposing to not be as others I considered worldly. Still, I did not have that personal and genuine walk with God (that many thought I had) until that day.

> *"He that dwelleth in the secret place of the Most*
> *High shall abide under the shadow of the Almighty."*
> Psalm 91:1 (KJV)

He didn't say to visit or drop by. He said dwell. Take up residence. Move in. Set up house with me. Let my presence permeate you, and I will change everything in your life from this day forward. There are some who need to be changed. You know Jesus, but you need to know the next step. You're asking, "Train me, God, for who I am to be." There are some who know about Jesus. There are some who used to know Jesus. There are some who have walked away from Jesus. There are some who simply forgot about this friend. But, He's not gone anywhere. He's still there beside you, simply waiting for you.

Remember our topic is "Redemptive Contextualization: Redemptive Missiology in Pneumatic Context." Maybe this event (this book) is a small part of Him permeating you and changing you for all He has for your life. It all has to do with a man's desire. David said,

> *"One thing have I desired of the Lord, that will I*
> *seek after..."* Psalm 27:4 (KJV)

The Holy Spirit REDEEMS that which DWELLS in Him. Too many people are unwilling to "dwell." Too many people have a "saving knowledge" of Jesus Christ but forget that they don't get saved on knowledge. You get saved on faith! We must remember that pneumatic redemptive missiology contextually recognizes the Holy Spirit's redeeming power of the call of God.

Giving knowledge to people will not show true love to the unlovable. Giving them what we know about the Bible will not show love to our neighbor, our family members, or the lost next door or down the street. What we need to be going after is an impartation of the Holy Spirit: not of man but God.

> "It all has to do with a man's desire."

Every person has specific needs. For you to be able to sense the needs of that person you must be moved by compassion and have sensitivity to the Holy Spirit and His presence. And, the only way to get compassion is to ask God for it. Our context is missions. We want to see our friends, our neighbors, our families and loved ones find Christ and His salvation power. Every person you meet, you know, or you encounter at the grocery, at the

> "You must be moved by compassion and have sensitivity to the Holy Spirit and His presence."

metro, at the plaza, when you eat at a restaurant, when you travel back to your home...

I've heard it said that people have three universal convictions:

1.  Hopelessness.
    The vast amount of individuals in the world are disheartened and without hope. In various manners their lives are falling apart, whether family, money, jobs, children, health… They're discouraged, hopeless, friendless, rejected, and feeling worthless.

    In the US, I was recently at a conference; many of you recognize the war on terror. The US is involved in that war. September 11, 2001, changed our country when the two largest towers in our nation fell by terrorists airplanes. At this conference, they spoke of American soldiers that had died in this war since 2001, and of some more than 8,000 who have died in battle. Shocking was the number then addressed— the over 200,000 who have died to suicide during or after returning from their military duty. We need to feel that…to meet it.

    > *"The vast amount of individuals in the world are disheartened and without hope."*

    William Booth, the founder of the Salvation Army said, "Find a hurt and heal it. Find a need and meet it." People are discouraged. They may look strong, they may look battle-worn, they may have the weapons of the world—it might be my brother or yours. They are strong or mighty, the one in our family who became the warrior. But, inside them you do not know their hurts or their pain. O God, give us eyes to see, hearts to feel. Let us feel as You feel, and Holy Spirit draw us to the hurts that I might bring them hope. Because God is a saving God—a good God—He is our today and our tomorrow.

2. Guilt.

People feel guilt-ridden; they feel judged; they feel unlovable, unacceptable, and not deserving of good blessings or favor to be upon their lives. They feel shame—maybe over a specific issue in their lives (we know it as sin)...or, abortion, various failures...or they've hurt someone.

> *"People feel guilt-ridden; they feel judged; they feel unlovable, unacceptable, and not deserving of good blessings or favor to be upon their lives."*

They will not tell you, but you must know every person can be touched by the Holy Spirit.

I call it "redemptive missiology in pneumatic context." Let me walk in the secret place, O God, so when I see, I do not see with my eyes but with my

25

heart. The Holy Spirit's heart of compassion touches the sinner's heart and changes them for all eternity.

You should tell people: You qualify, You matter, You're important, You are also His child, He's waiting for you to come home and call Him Father. Jesus loved people, and it's evidenced by how He gave things—attention, care, and communicating with people.

3. The Fear of Death.
   People have a remarkable apprehension of dying and death. You and I don't have that. We know we're saved. But the world...they don't have that security and they don't know of that promise. That's how you love the unlovable, the unloved, the burdened, weary, and heavy-hearted. Tell them Jesus is the good news!

Let's talk about genuinely caring for people.

I've met a number of individuals who claim to be Christian but who quite simply do not seem to like people. And, maybe like yourself, I've met a number of people who would not proclaim to be Christian or living a Christian life but who deeply care about people—all

> *"Jesus loved people, and it's evidenced by how He gave."*

people—and it resonates and shows so brightly in their lives, speech, and actions. One doesn't have to be a Christian to care about people. But, imagine, if we could find those genuinely caring people and help them find the life-transforming and amazing grace of Christ personally, how powerful and permeating their care and concerns for others would be in Christian service and witness!

The present general superintendent of the Assemblies of God, Doug Clay, recently spoke by my invitation at a leadership forum in my home state of Kentucky. He drove home the point that God's people need to be encouragers. We need to be telling people: You're important. You belong. You're needed. You qualify. Jesus loves you. We are to be about fulfilling the needs of those around us. Tell them truth; that sets men free.

JESUS loved people, demonstrated by His bountiful giving of three things:
1. Attention
2. Care
3. Communication

Have you ever been in a meeting or church service and while shaking people's hands their eyes are looking all around or beyond you, trying to see who might be more important or who else they should shake hands with? I certainly have. And I don't like it when it happens to me.

When missions is not a program, but your heart—as the heartbeat of God—you no longer look at anyone else. You look only at them; your heart goes nowhere else. And, it is from your heart, not a planned scheme. If there are others who want to talk to you, they'll wait, but for now your heart is focused. When you live like that the world will recognize it. You'll draw people to the presence of the Lord. They'll want to be more like you. They'll want to be close to you. They will see that you genuinely care, because... you do.

> *"We must first speak of our own brokenness, and then we must discern the needs."*

Consider these seven ways to discern people's needs. It is missions. How do we draw people to the presence of the Lord? We must first speak of our own brokenness, and then we must discern the needs. And, how do you discern the needy, the weary, the lost, the fearful, the ones Jesus would have you reach?

SEVEN WAYS to Distinguish and Recognize Needs:
1. Their countenance
2. Their eyes
3. People who are all alone
4. People who keep their head down
5. People who are new
6. People who are unkempt; a bit "different"
7. People who "sit in the back"

Maybe they've come to CTS (or if reading this, wherever you are) and they have no one. "They will be my friend," you say. You look for it. Christ died for them. They just haven't had the privileges you've had; they don't think they qualify. O, But He's a good, good Father. Church, pray. Pray the Holy Spirit inclines your heart as you dwell in His presence daily in your journeys. I heard it said once, "A ministry that is college-trained, but not Spirit-filled, works no miracles."

Why is missions important? A Christian father and a Christian stepmother had raised me. I had attended churches since my youth. I had chosen to avoid alcohol, mind-altering drugs, and tobacco of any kind. Do you know how many problems come into our life when we forget who's seated on the throne? I still forgot. I have family members who I love so deeply, but who I think forgot. I have friends who forgot.

People across the globe worship many things: the sun, the earth, the moon, false gods, charismatic leaders... I've been guest to mosques in both the United States and internationally where worship was to Muhammad. I've stood at the Western Wall in Jerusalem among faithful Jewish worshipers who, obligated to conduct tefillah

> "There's no guidepost to have to live up to. We do what we want. Period."

(prayer), pray not to Jesus, Messiah, but Hashem, "the Name," Adonai. I've been with many who worship nothing. In the USA, it's been said we worship ourselves. People feel there's no authority they answer to. There's no guidepost to have to live up to. We do what we want. Period.

Why is missions important? I say, because men are yet to be broken...and men are yet to be saved.

In my home near Louisville, Kentucky, I placed in my notes the call of Isaiah to missions work. His call came in Isaiah 6:1–13. He cried, "I am undone." Spurgeon said, God will not use a man He has not first undone. Isaiah recognized his own depravity. He saw himself before a holy God. Have you ever seen yourself that way? How many today would be willing to say, "I'm undone"?

> "His call came in Isaiah 6:1–13. He cried, 'I am undone.'"

Draw me, God, today. Because, Father, I say to You, Here am I. I'll go. Send me.

My challenge to you: be a voice.

Count Zinzendorf said, "I have but one passion—it is He, it is He alone. The world is the field and the field is the world; and henceforth that country shall be my home where I can be most used in winning souls for Christ."

The Lord said, "Go, and tell this people" (Isa. 6:9, KJV). Our society is under-challenged. Challenge people to change. So, as I close, I challenge you today:

- Be a voice as one crying in the wilderness, to today's Church, as lukewarm-ness and complacency overtake God's people.
- Ask God to break you—that you might be useful to Him and His work.
- Walk in humility, regardless of where God takes you.
- Hunger for God's presence. Redemption power comes from the secret place of the Holy Spirit.
- Ask God for discernment as you look for the needy and their needs so that redemption might flow through you.

I have constant reminders...of the One who gave me strength, gave me hope, gave me Renee and the two most precious gifts I've ever had—my two children.

Some of you are separated from your families; it's hard. Some of you have children. I would die a thousand times over for my children. That's how Jesus thought about me. So, He went to a cross to give me life and...trust me...He's given me a life more abundantly. He's calling some of you to a changed life. You're studying theology, but He's calling you to brokenness—that you might change lives.

O God, give me eyes to see, a heart to feel, that I might change a life. Only in discernment can you know to whom, when, and where you will be used for Him.

> *"I would die a thousand times over for my children. That's how Jesus thought about me. So, He went to a cross to give me life."*

Find a place to seek His face. Ask Him to break you—and to make us a voice.

## Section Two

Missional Pneumatology of God's Command: Why Should Churches Be Missions Sending Churches?

When I previously pastored a local congregation, we would have a large number of missionary guests with us in our church services. It became the norm. And, we received a good number of missionary offerings. It, too, became the norm.

Today, when I challenge churches to give—many of you may not have the money to give—you need to recognize it comes from that history. It was not uncommon in the last years of our pastorate some years ago to have 20, 30, and—up to the last year—likely 40 or more missionary guests in our services in that year's timeframe. The people of our church were incredible and had caught a personal heart for missions themselves. When you only have 52 weeks, that can be a challenge, having that many missionary guests. I know. Those of you in the ministry or who are pastors are saying to yourselves, "That's crazy." From this, you can also under-stand that when I hear a pastor tell me they host two or three missionaries a year, boastfully as if they are wonderfully missions equip-ping to their congregation, I smile, typically thinking to myself, but never saying it, "How I wish you could have your blinders removed so you could walk in that next level of faith for missions..."

> *"The people of our church were incredible and had caught a personal heart for missions themselves."*

But, that being, you see why I would often tell our church that while we were going to be regularly welcoming missionaries and receiving special offerings for their global works, I would continue to preach our services week to week. To do this, every missionary would share a fifteen-minute window, or less. And, every one, every time—week after week after week—when the missionary finished, I would step up and place my arm around the missionary in front of the audience. (Now, I only suggest you do that if it's contextually accepted. Know your audience and your missionary guest.) And, I would say this to my people:

*"I love you. And many of you gave last week. Many of*

*you gave again the week before that. Many of you give out of plenty. Many of you give out of poverty. And, I recognize you can't give every single time. But, I believe in this missionary and all I'm asking you to do is what the Holy Spirit tells you to do. You're a missions-faithful people. You believe in the work of Christ around the world. For most here, a gift of $10, or $25, or $50, will not impact whether or not your family eats this week or whether or not your family's needs are met. For some, it might. And, I encourage you to do only what the Holy Spirit directs of you. For some, you can't give, but you can pray. So, let's receive an offering."*

Week after week after week—how many times can you ask people for money?—and this was after we'd already received the tithes in the church. Week after week $500,

> *"All I'm asking you to do is what the Holy Spirit tells you to do."*

$800, $1,000, $2,000, (I think it was Missionary, David Grant who came to speak and his offering received was over) $8,000, ...the money would just continue. I don't know where it comes from. But, I know it's not about money. It's about brokenness. The Spirit of the Lord breaking a heart so we might hear from Him. And, when He breaks my heart, He...Can have it...All. Because, whatever I have is His. Wherever I go belongs to Him. And, when God says go, you go. When He says give, you give.

How much do you believe in the power of the God who's called you? So they would continue to give...from their hearts...it just flowed. What memories those years offer to me now.

We all have personal memories. I've also learned through the years we all process our own memories through our own lens. I suppose if I were to ask my siblings how they remember certain same incidents, they too would process it through their own perceptions, evalua-

> *"I know it's not about money. It's about brokenness. The Spirit of the Lord breaking a heart so we might hear from Him."*

tions, and viewpoints. Here's some of my story—from my lens.

I was between two and four years old when I remember my first real memories—hard memories for me. I am 56 years old at the time of this writing, and there are still times those memories will return like a flood. Memories of my biological - my maternal - mother entertaining men in my home when my father was away at work are as vivid as if it was yesterday. When I was six years old, that Christmas my father, who raised four children on a teacher's small salary (at the time) of $9,000 US per year, had spent a lot of his money (apparently) and purchased my mother a beautiful red dress. I remember that red dress. My memory is vivid of that particular day. It was Christmas. The big Christmas gift at our home as a child was a long and tantalizingly thick candy cane. You can't find those now as they were then in the late 1960s. My oldest brother, fourteen years my senior, bought me a similar one for Christmas this past year. It brought back memories. Annually, how I loved and waited to see the candy cane. So I remembered those days and the excitement of it all.

That particular Christmas my father was excited to give my mother that gift, I'm sure. Though I can't remember his emotion or sentiments, I can imagine it was supposed to be a special gift. I recall her opening it. She sat on the front side of our television family room in the small white frame home. I was seated (I think with my sister) on the opposite.

> "I remember that red dress. My memory is vivid of that particular day."

I had a full view of the scene. Then, it happened. I remember a huge argument on Christmas day, hands flailing, arms swinging: wrong size, wrong color, just wrong. She tore her dress and threw it back at my father. That's the home I grew up in. I could tell you many more memories, but this is one that gives you a good picture of the early days.

About six months later it was their 25th wedding

anniversary. Let me give a little more history. I was a late bloomer—a child well into their marriage, the fourth child. My father, a devoted Christian and faithful and loyal Baptist, wrote me a letter years later after I had entered the ministry, telling me of his disappointment in my religious choices in life. I still have that letter dated from October of 1988. In it, he acknowledged that he didn't know how he'd failed to get his spiritual ideas across to me and admitted I was the child, he said, of his older age. My father had told me just a few years before his passing (2004) that my mother had self-aborted a child the year before I was born. It was an event never spoken of during the years I was being raised. Apparently, it was something that had been kept silent, almost secretive even from the immediate family, and the feelings and emotions of it had been dormant all those years for various reasons. He went on to explain to me that when she got pregnant again, just a year later, she decided to keep this baby. I'm glad she did. I honor her. And, on their 25th anniversary, my father came home from work that day and his gift was a hand-signed card sitting on the table. It offered the simple sentiments that "We've had enough of this. I want a divorce and I've left," or something to that effect.

Other than just a few visits—following her leaving our home when I was six years old—I rarely ever saw my mother again. When my mother was dying years later, I was already a pastor. Two of my older siblings called me and said, "We know you don't really know her, but out of respect we felt it important to tell you your mother is in the hospital and likely dying tonight." It was about 1:00 o'clock in the morning. I was in bed. I leaned over to Renee and said I must go. So I got dressed and made the roughly three-hour drive to the city and hospital where she lay. When I arrived, those there seemed shocked to see my arrival. And, oddly, when I went back to where she was roomed, as if everyone knew she and I needed some time and space, the room cleared almost immediately.

> *"It was about 1:00 o'clock in the morning. I was in bed. I leaned over to Renee and said I must go."*

So, I went beside my mother, who could not speak but could hear. And it may sound strange, but I introduced myself to her. "I've done ok, Mom. You know I'm a pastor now..." She was my mother. She had kept up with me. "You know I married my college sweetheart and I have two beautiful children. Mom, I tell you—my God is faithful, and whatever you're carrying here tonight, Mom—I've come for one thing—to release you, to forgive you, to let you know God has taken care me, your child, and I come to encourage you, Mom—to know my Jesus so someday we can catch up on all the things we've missed." The doctors assured me she heard me, though she couldn't look at me and couldn't speak. My hope of hope is that she made things right with her God and that I will see her in heaven.

We must realize, Church, if we genuinely have a heart for missions, then we will love all people at all times and judge no one. You're not walking in their shoes. You don't know why they make the decisions they make. I don't know why my mother would have left me and her other children. I don't judge her. It's more common for fathers to leave children, unfortunately. It's horrific, but more common. But I'm convinced, Church...now bear with me...contextualize

> *"Love all people at all times and judge no one."*

with me...they're not just unsaved, they're lost. Your friends and loved ones are not just unsaved. They're lost. My topic is the missional pneumatology of God's command. And I define that as, Why should churches be missions sending churches?

Certainly, my motivation is this, and they go with me everywhere I go. (I showed the audience in Brussels a photo in my Bible of my family.) We all have to have a reason for living, and when your family is your reason it gives you purpose and challenges your call.

My challenge: In the next hour or so that I speak, whatever next step God shows you related to missions, will you be willing to submit? Whatever God is asking of you to do, will you do it? I ask you to pray this at the beginning of this message so that at the end of the message, you will know what you are committing to. You can pray now...

*It might mean praying, researching, giving, or going...but whatever next step God shows you, would you be willing to obey? Never worry about small beginnings.

> *"Do not despise these small beginnings, for the Lord rejoices to see the work begin."* Zech. 4:10 (NLT)

Most all of us have small beginnings. After all, you have no money. You have no major networks or course or direction. You may be saying, "I'm young. How can I do what I feel God's calling me to do?"

Look at Moses. He began his powerfully wide deliverance ministry with a mere shepherd's staff. Or, Elijah's cloud of rain... that began, in 1 Kings 18, appearing merely the size of a man's hand. Or, David and his kingship beginning with a sling shot and 5 stones (1 Sam. 17). Or, Zerubbabel's plum line (measuring line) to build the temple (Zech. 4:10). Or, Nehemiah rebuilding Jerusalem, beginning with the cup he willingly and obediently served to a pagan king (Neh. 2:1). Are you willing to serve?

Are you willing to only be handed a staff, when all you have are your hands to serve, and the ones you're serving are pagan? Are you willing to say, "Here am I. Send me. I will serve them, so that some of You, Lord, might rub off"?

So, be aware of the slightest of signs, the smallest of signs or wonders from God. God is in the details. And He will show Himself faithful.

> "*Whatever God is asking of you to do, will you do it?*"

Let's define the Great Commission Church:

The congregation and the pastor are committed to reaching the lost—at all costs—here and abroad, the ends of the earth. To pastor a missional church, these things are essential.

I was privileged to have lunch with the CTS (Continental Theological Seminary) missions committee. We discussed that every pastor should have a prayer team and a missions team. Nothing else matters but we being in His presence and that we reach the lost.

> "*God is in the details. And He will show Himself faithful.*"

What about giving? Remember faith giving is not how much is in our checkbook, on our card, or what's in our account. It's what you don't own. It's what you don't have. It's your giving in faith. Without God it can't happen. If you've chosen a dream that you can accomplish yourself, then it's not a God-sized dream. You don't need God to accomplish something you can do yourself. Dream big and dream God-sized dreams. So don't worry about what you have or don't have. God has all you need.

Paul Brannan, distinguished 50-plus-year missionary servant, taught me years ago of five essential elements of a Great Commission Church:

First, the church must have an active missions team. Second, it must have an annual or semi-annual missions emphasis with a system to raise support for missions (Faith Promise Challenges). Third, the church needs a well-planned monthly Missions Sunday (or whenever the church meets) service. Fourth to consider, regular and frequent prayer for missions and missionaries is a definite. And, finally, as I've spoken of already, an essential for a Great Commission Church is to welcome and host frequent missionary speakers.

> *"So don't worry about what you have or don't have. God has all you need."*

Why does it matter? Why should every church strive to be a Great Commission Church? Let's look at eight reasons.

1. Because Missions is our Heritage. Missions was a principle motive for organizing the AG. The AG committed the movement to the primary task of

43

evangelizing the world. "...We commit ourselves and this movement to God for the greatest evangelism the world has ever seen." Hot Springs, Arkansas, 1914— about 300 people gathered, argued, fasted, and prayed 3 days. The AG was formed in unity under the umbrella of the 16 Tenets of Faith. Committed to world evangelization from the very beginning. And, we must be a missions giving church...

2.      Because Much of the Task Remains to Be Done. We rejoice that the AG (Pentecostals worldwide) are the largest evangelical missions movement in the world. We are thrilled to see the rapid growth, currently about 68 million AG members and adherents, not counting China, a nation that ignores evangelical numbers. But the truth is that at least half of the world has yet to hear an adequate presentation of the gospel. The work is vast

> *"J. Philip Hogan, said, "We can't boast about the grain in the silos as long as there is still a harvest awaiting in the field."*

and the harvesters are few. There are far more people in the world today who have not had an adequate gospel witness than when we could ever imagine. A former director of missions for the AG, the late J.

Philip Hogan, said, "We can't boast about the grain in the silos as long as there is still a harvest awaiting in the field."

3.  Because the Church Is God's Only Method for Reaching the Whole Key Scripture for this lecture/message:

> *"The Church is God's only method. Christ has commanded the Church to reach the World. lost."*

> *"13 for, 'Everyone who calls on the name of the Lord will be saved.' 14 How, then, can they call on the one they have not believed in? And how can they believe in the one of whom they have not heard? And how can they hear without someone preaching to them? 15 And how can they preach unless they are SENT? As it is written: How beautiful are the feet of them who bring good news."* Romans 10:13-15 (NIV) emphasis mine.

4.  Because Christ Has Commanded Us to Reach the World. All four gospels include the Great Commission. Just before Christ went away, He left a promise and a command:

> *"But ye shall receive power, after that the Holy Ghost is come upon you: and ye shall be witnesses unto me both in Jerusalem, and in all Judaea, and in Samaria, and unto*

> *the uttermost part of the earth."* Acts 1:8
> (KJV)

The Church is God's only method. Christ has commanded the Church to reach the lost.

5. Because They Will Be Eternally Lost If We Fail to Warn Them.

   *"When I say to the wicked, 'You wicked person, you will surely die,' and you do not speak out to dissuade them from their ways, that wicked person will die for their sin, and I will hold you accountable for their blood."* Ezekiel 33:8 (NIV)

   It was Jesus's command that we reach the lost.
6. Because We Will Be Harshly Judged If We Fail to Reach the Lost with the Salvation Message.

   *"When I say to the wicked, 'You wicked person, you will surely die,' and you do not speak out to dissuade them from their ways, that wicked person will die for their sin, and I will hold you accountable for their blood."* Ezekiel 33:8 (NIV)

7. Because There Is Still Time to Obey Christ's Command. The Bible says in John 4:35,

   *"Look around you! Vast fields of human souls are ripening all around us, and are ready now for*

*reaping."* John 4:35 (TLB)

There's time to obey His command. And,

8. Because We Need One-Another to Make This Happen.

*"The harvest is so great, and the workers are so few. So pray to the one in charge of the harvesting, and ask him to recruit more workers for his harvest fields."* Matthew 9:37–38 (TLB)

Challenge: Who is God calling? Who is God challenging? He may be calling you to missional calls here or abroad or maybe in your home country. The harvest is now, ready, and it is great.

Global worker Steve Turley explained that Death Valley in the USA is not dead. In a recent year, Death Valley received as much rain in three or four hours as it typically receives in a year. The following spring, the valley floor was covered with flower blossoms. A gift from God and a reminder,

> *"The Harvest Is Now. The Harvest Is Ready. And, The Harvest Is Great."*

under the vast dead valley was life awaiting to be born and set free. What a powerful witness and testimony.

Whether it be missional endeavors here, abroad, in your home country...or the raising up of churches...or the seeing of revival...The Harvest Is Now. The Harvest Is Ready. And, The Harvest Is Great.

Let's spend a few minutes thinking about that: The Harvest Is Now.

> *"Do you think the work of harvesting will not begin until the summer ends four months from now? Look around you! Vast fields of human souls are ripening all around us, and are ready now for reaping."* John 4:35 (TLB)

We need workers now, willing to be in that secret place we've spoken of and to be ready for whatever and wherever He calls you. The harvest is ripe and it must be reaped now, or it will rot in the field.

When I lived life without my mother, I never even thought of it...I never dreamt there would ever be a day that I would sit and talk with her. But, at the end of her life—in her last hours—there I sat in what I considered an open door from the Lord sharing with her about how

> *"But, what if I had not gone? The harvest is ripe. It's ready. It's now. And it's urgent."*

I'd found a life-changing relationship with Christ, His hope, and how He'd watched over me my entire life. But, what if I had not gone? The harvest is ripe. It's ready. It's now. And it's urgent.

The Harvest Is Ready. Harvest time is always urgent. It does not wait for our convenience. It must be reaped when the harvest is ripe, or again, it will rot in the field. The world is ripe for the reapers of the Kingdom—or the pit.

I have a missionary friend, Dave Amsler, now in Guatemala, who was famous for saying an Assemblies of God young people's missions project called "Speed the Light" simply meant, "We get there first." The

> *"The mind and heart of the lost are just as ready to believe the devil's lie or the Lord's truth."*

reality is, fields are ripe for whomever arrives first. Sadly, blinded hearts and blinded eyes will receive false messages and false teachings if they are not first introduced to the Savior, Jesus Christ. The mind and heart of the lost are just as ready to believe the devil's lie or the Lord's truth.

Today is the day of harvest. And it's a great harvest.

1. It Is Great in Size. Some say over 4 billion people in the world have not heard of Jesus or His promises.

2. It Is Great in Urgency.

   *"How then shall they call on Him in whom they have not believed? and how shall they believe in*

> *Him of whom they have not heard? and how shall they hear without a preacher?"* Romans 10:14 (KJV)

Jesus said,

> *"Therefore pray the Lord of the harvest to send out [thrust forth] laborers into His harvest."* Matthew 9:38 (NKJV) addition in parenthesis mine.

3.  It Is Great in Value. These are immortal souls, made in the image of God and destined to live eternally. With the work of the Holy Spirit they are able to live in goodness and usefulness, love, joy, and peace to be introduced to redeeming grace. How will they know if no one tells them? We are not students simply to be students. We are here to change the world for Christ. The worst of them was worthy of the sacrifice of Christ's life and the shedding of His precious blood. No one should be lost.

> *"The Lord is not slow to fulfill His promise as some count slowness, but is patient toward you, not wishing that any should perish, but that all should reach repentance."* 2 Peter 3:9 (ESV)

4.  It Is Great in Difficulties. The harvest is a task impossible to man alone. Bonhoeffer spoke of a cheap grace. So, we must recognize that to those truly called

there will be challenges. Let us always remember,

*"Greater is he that is in you than he that is in the world." 1 John 4:4 (KJV)*

With God all things are possible.

> *"The worst of them was worthy of the sacrifice of Christ's life and the shedding of His precious blood."*

The worker is faced with a number of trials. The attacks of Satan; the prejudices of man; race, caste, politics, and religions; all the evil of centuries of corruption; the challenges of financing the work of God; all are at times overwhelming.

There is a lack of partners to bring in the harvest. In Matthew 9:38, the suggested context is "thrusting forth" laborers into the harvest. That was the prayer requested of Jesus. He was not simply praying for a harvester. His prayer had already occurred and He was thrusting harvesters into the harvest. Might we say, "Lord send me. Lord thrust me. Send me now."

If we speak of thrusting forth, we should frame it in two phases: going and sending.

I think the American church is primarily a consumer church, but there's a big difference in the missional church. The consumer church is seen as a dispenser of religious

51

goods and services. People come to church to be "fed," to have their needs met through quality programs, and to have the professionals teach their children about God. The missional church is a body of people sent on mission who gather in community for worship, community encouragement, and teaching from the Word in addition to what they are feeding themselves throughout the week. It's the difference of "I go to church" versus "I am the church." Missional churches come together as a body and bring Jesus with them when they come. Amazing things happen. It's a church of world-changers. And those people will change the world.

> *"If we speak of thrusting forth, we should frame it in two phases: going and sending."*

> *"Senders understand there is money and prayers in their sacrifice."*

"Goers" will involve a great army of volunteers, young and old alike, who are willing to leave home and family to reach around the globe with the message of hope. Their commitment to the task must be without conditions. Nothing will stop them from pushing back the darkness with the Light of the world.

A sender, on the other hand, is quite obviously one who is not a goer. Some can go; others send. Senders understand there is money and prayers in their sacrifice.

When my children were in college, my wife and I would regularly fill a box full of candy, snacks of various kinds, simple small gifts, and items that—if for no other reason—simply said, "We miss you, and we love you." It took some time to gather things. It took some money to buy the things. And, it took some effort to package it up, wrap and tape it carefully, drive it to the nearest post office, and mail it. Then, I'd pull out a credit card and smile as the post office official weighed the box, telling me it would be $15, or more, to mail it. But not one time was there a sense of remorse or wishing I hadn't done it. Rather, I wanted to do it all the more and send a larger box next time. Why? I understood something. They were my kids. I loved them deeply. I missed them genuinely. I couldn't go be with them. But, I could SEND my heart and prayers to them, through that box.

> *"I understood something. They were my kids. I loved them deeply."*

Senders understand their calling involves a great outpouring of money and prayers in a spirit of mag-nificent giving and self-sacrifice. Those who remain at home must be as committed in their sending of missionaries as the missionaries are in their going.

*Missio Dei* is a Latin Christian theological term that can be translated as the "mission of God," or the "sending of

God." *Missio Dei* thrusts you into His harvest because the lost are not simply unsaved, they're lost. The harvest is great. It is ready. And it is now. He's calling people to not just be consumer Christians but involved and active followers. There's a world of difference in knowing the Word of God and knowing the God of the Word. When you know the God of the Word, you can't help but want to go, or want to send. It's in the Christian's DNA.

We said in the first main session that the calling in Ephesians is for the church to fulfill its role in the mission of God, to participate in the *missio Dei*. G. Van Rheenan said, "God's mission flows from God to Christ to the Holy Spirit, who empowers the church, who carries on the mission to the world" (Eph. 1:10).

> *"When you know the God of the Word, you can't help but want to go, or want to send. It's in the Christian's DNA."*

A Christian mission is an organized effort to spread Christianity. Missions often involves sending individuals and groups, called missionaries— or more commonly today, "Workers"— across boundaries, for the Kingdom purposes of humanitarian aid, apostolic planting of churches, the developing of Christo-centric agencies and ministries, and direct or indirect proselytism (the conversion to Christianity from non- or post-Christian traditions). Yes, I believe in

Jesus. And, yes, I believe in proselytism (as it is generally understood). I want all to know Jesus and understand His amazing grace and promises. How can they know unless someone tells them?

> *I want all to know Jesus and understand His amazing grace and promises."*

> *"The people that do know their God shall be strong, and do exploits."*

God is to do the work of salvation and restoration, and the church is to bear witness to it. And, the mission of the church is the mission of Christ ...because the church is of Christ.

> *"When I am gone, say nothing about William Carey—speak only about William Carey's Saviour."*
> William Carey

> *"You have one business on earth—to save souls."*
> John Wesley

> *"I have but one passion: It is He, it is He alone. The world is the field and the field is the world; and henceforth that country shall be my home where I can be most used in winning souls for Christ."*
> Count Nicolaus Ludwig von Zinzendorf

We said earlier, there is a world of difference between knowing the Word of God and knowing the God of the

Word. We also talked about the fact that it's not what you know these days that matters, but Whom you know.

> *"The people that do know their God shall be strong, and do exploits."* Daniel 11:32 (KJV)

Men need to be a pillar of fire. They need to be God-guided men to lead a mistaken and ill-advised people. Are you God-guided? Is that you? Are you willing to be the only one in your family or the only one in your workplace…the only one in your school…the only one in your church to say, "Send me, I will go." I sat at a luncheon recently with a wonderful gentleman. He was a thirty-something immigrant from Mexico who explained to me he was the only one in his immediate family that knew Jesus. I was challenged by his faith and his dedication amidst the challenges of his own familial upbringing and relationships. Are you willing to accept His call? Are you willing to lose some of the joys of life today?

I lost my whole life with my mother for today's hope that I will have eternity with my maternal mother. Are you willing to recognize the call as a sacrifice? With God all things are possible.

The Holy Spirit is calling leaders to raise a standard. A standard is a holy work. It is a spiritual work. And one of the problems of the American church is they have few standards. I can't speak to the Belgian church—or the

French—or the Congolese—but I can speak to the American Church. Never—or rarely—challenged to do anything, their standards are too low.

I used to say, "Young ladies, wear your virtue as a crown, and young men, wear your honor as a sword." We need to challenge the church today. And the church needs to be challenged to reach the lost. They need to be challenged to be givers—generous givers in total faith that God will provide. And He'll provide more than you can even imagine or think. We need inspired men for today's church. Are you inspired to reach to today's church?

> "The Holy Spirit is calling leaders to raise a standard."

Dr. Dimitrov, president of Continental Theological Seminary here in Brussels, spoke in a recent Spiritual Emphasis of the school about primitive pneumology: "The work of the Holy Spirit is holy and spiritual." Inspired men are desperately needed in today's church, and inspiration is imparted in prayer.

In Luke 10:2, Christ shows us the source from which needs are supplied by the mandate of ...*pray the Lord of the harvest*... God's plan for world evangelization can only occur with the Holy Spirit's prayer and power. Nothing makes it possible for the human mantle or effort except through prayer. Prayer will reach workers with a heavenly call. It will send forth workers, the right kind of workers. It will train workers in God's school of pneumatology. It will send them to the right fields. It will also sustain them when they go.

Is that you? ... Prayer will sustain you when you go! It will keep you strong wherever you are and give you hope when you're alone. Prayer will supply the needed finances to

> *"Inspired men are desperately needed in today's church, and inspiration is imparted in prayer."*

do whatever He's called you to do. Prayer will remove mountains, challenges, and roadblocks. And, your time in the secret place will remove the barriers and difficulties. Prayer will break down barriers.

D. L. Moody said, *"A man who prays much in private will make short prayers in public."*

Author Max Lucado said, *"The power of prayer is not in the one praying, but in the One who hears our prayers."*

Prayer is the undergirding of the Church. It is the undergirding of everyone who feels and senses the call to missions. It is the undergirding of all called to be great pastors and pastoral leaders. Confessing you're not prepared well to pray or thinking you've not developed that discipline very well is exactly how we should reason. Some super-Christians teach "a true believer" will spend that hour a day, or that "this or that." That's a wonderful commitment and a commended discipline for those who have developed the routine and intimacy with God. But, for most, simply acknowledging where we are, humbly and honestly before the Father, is the perfect place to start. God's love for you, His love for His children, and His desire for you and me, is that we will quite simply "dwell in Him." Don't worry about spending the hour or the half-hour, or the "whatever." Let your heart and mind be dwelling in His presence and in communion with Him at all times. The thirty-minute commute to and from work can be an intimate time with the Lord. While you're in the middle of a challenging conversation with a colleague, your heart and mind can be "stayed on Him" and, essentially, be dwelling simultaneously in prayerful communion with the Father.

> *"Prayer will remove mountains, challenges, and roadblocks. And, your time in the secret place will remove the barriers and difficulties."*

Weeks after I had whole-heartedly-given my heart and life to the Lord during my university days, I was driving from my dorm each Sunday morning, alone, to attend church. I remember it as if it were yesterday when the officer said to me, "Young man, you're lucky to be alive. You've totaled that lady's car, and this telephone pole. Your car is drivable but I wouldn't suggest you take it very far.

What exactly were you doing when you ran that red light and hit her car?" "I was driving to church. I was praying, Sir." He looked at me with that puzzled look. I mean, seriously, how many college students early on Sunday mornings are driving to church and praying? He didn't say very much, looking at the documents he was writing regarding the accident. He responded with a simple, "I suggest you pray with your eyes open next time," and walked away.

> *"Don't worry about spending the hour or the half-hour, or the "whatever." Let your heart and mind be dwelling in His presence and in communion with Him at all times."*

So, it is very possible to be multi-tasking and praying simultaneously. Be in prayer, friends. But, if you're driving...pray with your eyes open.

I've told Kentucky AG churches many times, an Assemblies of God church that does not support missions should take the name off the door, because missions is not a program. It is the very heart of God. There is no other reason for a church's existence, but that we would reach the lost—at all cost.

Our time together is but a fleeting vapor preparing us for a time that we will stand in the presence of the King of kings. We desire to hear Him say, "Well done, good and faithful servant..." I can't wait for my mom to hear that, for your families to hear that, for my father, my stepmother, my sister... But, there's still time for others who do not know, have not heard, and are yet to humble themselves just enough to accept the love of the Father. The harvest is great. It's ripe. It's ready. And, He's calling you now.

How many believe my mother who left me as a child still loved me and her children? I believe. I have to. It's how I survived. In spite of things that were said, or things that were done... or not said, or not done. I believe. Now, I might actually know a bigger picture to this analogy, but in context, all I can do is trust and believe for the best. The Bible says, "If there is anything of good report, think on these things." So, I try to live in the positive. And, with that view of life's journeys, what mother doesn't

> *"There is no other reason for a church's existence, but that we would reach the lost— at all cost."*

internally love her children? Do you think in that last hour of her life she listened to what I said? I think she did. Why? Because she loved. But, "She left him," you say. Her life was challenged. Have any of you had challenges? It's not always easy, but as followers of Christ, we must pray His compassions—that never fail—be blanketed over us, first and foremost. For we are the ones in need of His touch, His

61

forgiveness, and His mercies.

So, for you, remember, your family loves you. Pray the Lord of the harvest—in the secret place—to tell you at what time to go share with them the gospel of hope. Though they may say they do not, in their heart of hearts they love you and they will hear you. And then, remember you're not God. Let the Holy Spirit do His work. We are merely servants and vessels. The voice of God, His hands and feet extended, the Bible says.

> *"Not by might, nor by power, but by my Spirit, says the Lord of Hosts."* Zechariah 4:6 (ESV)

Jesus left only one prayer request. Shouldn't we give it top priority?

> *"Then He said to them, 'The harvest truly is great, but the laborers are few; therefore pray the Lord of the harvest to send out laborers in His harvest.'"* Luke 10:2 (NKJV)

Let me now turn my thoughts to the Holy Spirit's anointing. May we never forget it's the anointing that breaks chains and every yoke of bondage. The Church today leans toward man's gifts. Christian leaders should never be confused with "these ways that seem right to a man…"

The Church must embrace altogether the talents and gifts designed and given by God as empowered and directed by the Holy Spirit!

I've been in churches where the most incredible talent is on the platform. Many, many, albums, CDs, music—wonderful and great stuff. Some of them also have the anointing. Many are putting out great genius. But, let's not forget, there's a great need for more than talent. We've a need for an anointed group of Pentecostal leaders in today's world. And, we have a need for well-versed, studied and doctrinally sound, anointed leaders for the Church. I didn't say anything about a particular denomination or organization. I didn't say one couldn't be a part of whatever church you're a part of (as long as you're in a church that preaches Bible truth and the Jesus of the Scripture).

> *"Jesus left only one prayer request. Shouldn't we give it top priority?"*

But, the reality is, Pentecostalism is far broader than a denomination or organization. Catholics, Baptists, Presbyterians, Methodists, Independents, Episcopalians, Nazarenes, and hundreds of other fellowships across the globe have men and women filled with the Holy Spirit and walking in the power and witness of Pentecost.

> *"Pentecostalism is far broader than a denomination or organization."*

Think of those Christian leaders who are not called to pulpit or church ministry. I believe the future of the Church could be bright with the addition of primarily non-pulpit ministry community leaders, called of God, and officially commissioned and endorsed by worldwide movements to work globally in the corporate world for the glory of God. Some call it marketplace ministry. I believe today's culture will not be transformed until every segment of society is permeated with the faith of the elect.

God's command to *Go Ye Therefore* is not isolated to cathedrals and churches, but to the whole world that they might know Him and the power of His resurrection. There is a great need for an anointed generation of Pentecostal leaders. There's a vacuum of what Leonard Ravenhill said was a lost art, the art of "Soul Hot Preaching." A sermon born

> *"I believe the future of the Church could be bright with the addition of primarily non-pulpit ministry community leaders, called of God, and officially commissioned and endorsed."*

in the head is simply that. It reaches the head. But a sermon born in a man or woman's heart reaches another's heart. It is transformative. It impacts others.

Unction cannot be learned. It is only received in the secret place of prayer—only earned by prayer. Victories are not won through sermons being preached in the pulpit by clergy or preachers alone, but in the prayer closets and secret place relationships of the faithful. And, there really is no secret in praying. The secret is what's been said for centuries—praying in secret. Still, and in no way lessening the calling of God for the preaching ministry, there is a shifting global culture that has opened numerous platforms to share Christ in ways never before conceived.

Today, the fellowship denomination of my spiritual covering is sending missionaries who are teachers, lawyers, doctors, workers, computer technicians, architects, financiers, and trained people from every walk of life into missionary service. There are many countries of the world that no longer let a preacher into their nations. My own daughter holds a masters in social work and is leaving within months to serve in Latin America. There are countries and ministries that would believe a minister or a preacher to not have the credentials necessary to be allowed for that country's entry, but a man or woman in the secret place—who carries talents, gifts, skills and is called by God— God is opening doors one after another. So a man or woman can change the world. Just have ears to hear His voice. He is calling. He is speaking to those who will hear. It is God himself who is the author of apostolic creativity. If you can think it, through the Spirit's directives, you can do it.

> *"There is a shifting global culture that has opened numerous platforms to share Christ in ways never before conceived."*

Knowing that, there is a difference between gifts and anointing. "Gifts amuse. Gifts may fascinate. Gifts may captivate, mesmerize, charm, or intrigue." Australian evangelist Christine Caine said this and more, continuing with the message that "gifts fill rooms and gifts stir people up..." but the Bible says in Isaiah 10:27, it is the Anointing that breaks chains and bondages'; breaks burdens and releases captives... and it only comes through crushing—those often times devastating, sometimes humiliating, overwhelming moments of defeat, sense of failure, or the lowest points of your journey.

> "It is God himself who is the author of apostolic creativity. If you can think it, through the Spirit's directives, you can do it."

*The yoke –the burden of the anti-christ- will be broken because of the anointing; not because of giftings or talent or oratory skill –but anointing. And, since the reference is the destruction of the antichrist – and the bible says the Messiah will destroy Him – Jesus is the anointing – it's all about Jesus.* Isaiah 10:21

Where we are so defeated and crushed and Jesus is our only chance, our only hope, or anchor, it's there where the oil of anointing survives. We have a global generation that refuses to be crushed but wants to be announced, postured, and admired. As long as that continues, the church will continue to have many who are gifted leaders but not anointed pastors, teachers, evangelists, prophets, or apostles.

> *"Where we are so defeated and crushed and Jesus is our only chance, our only hope, or anchor, it's there where the oil of anointing survives."*

God is looking for those willing to be crushed, new wine, broken, so His oil of anointing will be manifest. In your lowest moment, your darkest valley, He is there. I promise you, His promises of grace are sufficient:

*"Three times I pleaded with the Lord to take it away from me. But he said to me, 'My grace is sufficient for you, for my power is made perfect in weakness.' Therefore I will boast all the more gladly about my weaknesses, so that Christ's power may rest on me."* 2 Corinthians 12:8–9 (NIV)

*"God resists the proud, but gives grace to the humble."* James 4:6 (NKJV)

*"Grace and peace be yours in abundance through the knowledge of God and of Jesus our Lord."*

67

2 Peter 1:2 (NIV)

The anointed must choose to accept the call: the call to pastor, the call to send, the call to go, the call to pray. Let's remember our topic here. It's the missional pneumatology of God's command. Why should churches be missions sending churches?

> *"In your lowest moment, your darkest valley, He is there."*

> *"Your generation is the most passionate generation in the history of mankind."*

It's a common phrase for people to say in the United States: "The greatest churches are yet to be planted." But it's true. My generation is a baby boomer generation, but gen-Xers and millennial, gen-Y's, gen- Z's, and those who come thereafter if the Lord tarries, will win this world. Your generation is the most passionate generation in the history of mankind. Maybe your counterparts are not all believers but overall the world seems to be showing this millennial generation as compassionate and committed, even those who do not know Christ, to meet needs. They're compassionate to meet social needs. Show them a need and they want to meet it. And if you'll give them Jesus many will say, "Yes." But you have not because you ask not. And they do not now know Christ because no one has told them.

Reach this generation, friends. Reach this world. My

generation can't do it alone anymore. I beg of you, reach this world for Christ. Give your all for the Cross.

"I have nothing to give," you say. And, for the offering plate of your missions service as it goes by, you have nothing to give. Then,

> *"I believe the greatest MISSIONS PASTORS are yet to be released! Will you be one of them?"*

write on a piece of paper and drop this in: "I will give you my life." How many of you will give your life for the gospel?

I believe the greatest MISSIONS PASTORS are yet to be released! Will you be one of them? Not only is the Holy Spirit calling some to GO. As we've already spent some time addressing, He's calling some to SEND. The Spirit anoints and gifts individuals for His perfect plan for their lives.

> *"Be faithful friends. Purpose to not defile yourselves."*

> *"It does not take a great man to serve God, but it takes all of that man."* William Booth

There is no greater calling than to be used of God. Be faithful friends. Purpose to not defile yourselves. (Dan. 1:8).

Martin Luther had ten qualifications for the ministers in his organization. Look them over. They are still pertinent for today.

## Luther's 10 Qualifications for the Minister

1. He should be able to teach plainly and in order.
2. He should have a good head.
3. He should have good power of the language.
4. He should have a good voice.
5. He should have a good memory.
6. He should know when to stop.
7. He should be sure of what he means to say.
8. He should be ready to stake body, soul, goods, and reputation on Truth.
9. He should study diligently.
10. He should suffer himself to be vexed and criticized by everyone.

Finally, I want to offer an encouragement to the afflictions for "the Called." For those accepting the calling to ministry, the Spirit calls, but there are still battles. Remember, Paul wrote to the Ephesian church,

> *"We wrestle not against flesh and blood, but against principalities, against powers, against the rulers of the darkness of this world, against spiritual wickedness in high places"* Ephesians 6:12 (KJV)

So, what about the trials, the battles, and the sufferings?

Remember "But God."

*"But we have this treasure in jars of clay to show that this all-surpassing power is from God and not from us. 8 We are hard pressed on every side, but not crushed; perplexed, but not in despair; 9 persecuted, but not abandoned; struck down, but not destroyed. 10 We always carry around in our body the death of Jesus, so that the life of Jesus may also be revealed in our body. 11 For we who are alive are always being given over to death for Jesus' sake, so that his life may also be revealed in our mortal body. 12 So then, death is at work in us, but life is at work in you.*

*13 It is written: 'I believed; therefore I have spoken.' Since we have that same spirit of faith, we also believe and therefore speak, 14 because we know that the one who raised the Lord Jesus from the dead will also raise us with Jesus and present us with you to himself. 15 All this is for your benefit, so that the grace that is reaching more and more people may cause thanksgiving to overflow to the glory of God.*

*16 Therefore we do not lose heart. Though outwardly we are wasting away, yet inwardly we are being renewed day by day. 17 For our light and momentary troubles are achieving for us an*

71

> *eternal glory that far outweighs them all. 18 So we*
> *fix our eyes not on what is seen, but on what is*
> *unseen, since what is seen is temporary, but what*
> *is unseen is eternal."*
> 2 Corinthians 4:7–18 (NIV)

A child of God sees his or her faith strengthened through afflictions—and you can judge the afflictions as to how burdensome they might be, as to the time they impact us, and as to the impact or effect they make upon our lives.

I.   As to their burdens. God calls them "light afflictions." When we are going through them they seem anything but "light." And then, we find the deeper truth. They are truly "light" when evaluated in fair balances. When we consider what we deserve, or when we consider how deep others suffer, or when we consider the very sufferings Christ endured for our salvation and to make His impact on lives, we recognize the things we suffer are light in comparison.

II.  As to their time. They are only momentary, a fleeting vapor. Joseph didn't call those weary prison years "a moment." The captives in Babylon surely didn't call those years of hopelessness "a moment." It was in these brief seasons, though, unbearable pain agonized God's people. And, we can never call short those dreadful six hours of agony that Jesus was hanging on the Cross. Yet we find the deeper truth...in what He did...

III.   As to their influence—the power of that moment on your life—the hurt, the pain, the agonies, the tears, the loneliness, the burden, the wanting to throw in the towel...Paul said it's "working...a weight of glory" (2 Cor. 4:17, NKJV). It is as important that we should be prepared for glory as it is for glory to be prepared for us! Paul's idea of glory is what is done by affliction in the Christian himself, bringing him or her to a life of faith.

*"While we look not at the things which are seen, but at the things which are not seen: for the things which are seen are temporal; but the things which are not seen are eternal."*
2 Corinthians 4:18 (KJV)

God has commanded us to *Go Ye Therefore*—but it is only by the power of the Holy Spirit that lives will be changed, God's Church built, and the lost eternally saved. It is the missional pneumatology of God's command.

In our time together we'll be speaking about giving: the tithe, the offerings above, and faith giving—that moment of being totally dependent upon God to perform the miracle. Many today have those kinds of prayers—needs with family and in your life, miracles needed. It is by faith we see these miracles come about. So I challenge you today to commit now. Challenge yourself. Challenge your people to change the world. And, be world-changers.

Too many people believe happiness is our best goal in life. Commit to be a Great Commission Church—that they might know holiness. We are either goers or we are senders. Which are you?

> *"Too many people believe happiness is our best goal in life."*

Whatever you standards are, raise them now. Dr. Joseph Dimitrov's testimony was amazing. "Dad, do you not trust me? Yes, I trust you. ... But, (son) it's not 'if' the devil were to come knocking—it's 'when' he will arise."

Our society is under-challenged. Challenge people to change. So, as I close this teaching, I challenge you today:

- Commit Now: to be a Great Commission Pastor/Church.
- Determine Now: Are you a goer? Or a sender?
- Raise Now: Your standards.
- Don't Settle Now: For the gifted; be anointed.
- Purpose Now: To not defile yourself over the things

that are seen (Dan. 1:8).

- Remember Now: The things that are not seen are eternal!

There are more people alive today who have never heard the name of Jesus, and more people today alive than a year ago who have never heard. Only people who are God-conscious will change that. Remember, they are not just unsaved, they are lost.

> *"I always give a moment for those to whom I speak to respond in some manner to what we've discussed."*

Prayer: *Heavenly Father, what we are doing now is the work of the Kingdom. It's faith. As we make this commitment to you, we know it's not the money you're looking for. It's faith if we'll just believe in you. So Lord, this evening, may this be a great expression of faith.*

I always give a moment for those to whom I speak to respond in some manner to what we've discussed. In my circles it's often called an altar call. The altar call for this lecture is very specific and very simple. It is a call to missions... It is a call to say, "I'm willing to go." It is a call to say, "Here am I, send me." It is a call to say, "I'm willing to send." And maybe it is even a challenge and a call to give a year of your life so you can pray about a lifetime ahead. Some here already sense a call to missions. Others here—I believe the spirit is speaking to you to change your course. Remember, the harvest is ripe. It is ready. And it is now. *Here am I. Send me, Lord.* If that's you, spend some time with the Lord and accept that challenge.

## *Section Three*

Financial Contextualization of *Missio Dei*:
Financing the Mission of God

Jesus said to be a servant, give to others!

> *"Do nothing from selfishness or empty conceit, but
> with humility of mind let each of you regard one
> another as more important than himself; do not
> merely look out for your own personal interests,
> but also for the interests of others."* Philippians
> 2:3–4 (NASB 1977)

There are numerous attitudes and value systems floating around the world today. Let's consider some of them: Be yourself. Be wise. Be bold. Be strong. Be good. Be cunning. Be sexy. Be sensuous. Be resourceful. Be confident. Be satisfied. Be visionary. Be purposed. Be positive. Be flexible. Be time conscious. Be brave. Be intuitive. Be accepting. Be balanced. Be enthusiastic. And there's hundreds more.

I was at a wedding recently and some non-believers were talking about how the couple looked so happy. They said to the group, "No matter how you live, everyone deserves to be happy." Happy for the couple, I was also broken. I don't think God called any of us to mere happiness. He called us to holiness. The gospel promises the same to everyone who trusts in Christ. Freedom from bondage is a central theme of our Lord Christ. Wesley wrote, "My chains fell off, my heart was free, I rose, went forth, and followed thee." Jesus said... be a servant. Serve others. The Scripture likewise taught to be generous. Jesus said, be a servant. His word said, be generous. Help chains fall and followers rise.

> *"Wesley wrote, 'My chains fell off, my heart was free, I rose, went forth, and followed thee.'"*

Before one can grow churches to be generous givers, one must become, personally, a generous giver. We must build others up. We must serve others. We can no longer live to—and for—ourselves. We are God's servants.

Is this really biblical? By only looking at the New Testament, I'll let you determine that yourself.

> *"...give preference to one another...contributing to the needs of the saints..."* Romans 12:10–13 (NASB)

*"...and let us consider how to stimulate one another to love and do good deeds..."* Hebrews 10:24 (NASB)

*"...But we proved to be gentle among you...having thus a fond affection for you, we were well-pleased to impart to you not only the gospel of God but also our own lives...therefore encourage...build up one another..."* 1 Thessalonians 2:7–8, 5:11, (NASB 1977)

*"...but through love serve one another..."* Galatians 5:13 (NASB)

*"...For the love of Christ controls us, ...that one died for all ...and He died for all that they who live should no longer live for themselves but for Him who died and rose again on their behalf..."* 2 Corinthians 5:14–15 (NASB 1977)

*"...for we do not preach ourselves but Christ Jesus as Lord, and ourselves as your bond-servants for Jesus' sake."* 2 Corinthians 4:5 (NASB 1977)

We are first SERVANTS. Second Corinthians 8 describes best the answer to the question of, "How should servants give?"

Paul wrote concerning the giving of the Macedonian Christians when he said,

> *"For I testify that according to their ability, and beyond their ability, they gave of their own accord."* 2 Corinthians 8:3 (NASB)

Now, Paul was collecting money for a struggling church in Jerusalem. And, as he made his way through Macedonia, he found generous givers. What makes this passage amazing is that Macedonia was already an economically depressed area.

> *"We are first SERVANTS."*

It would be like the poorest communities of Europe going to the poorest communities of India or Africa and asking them to give money for the struggling church in that great walled city, the richest among them in the city of light, the city called Jerusalem. Or, it would be like the poorest communities asking the poorest if they would give to the poorest.

Your needs are not about money. They're about faith. And, about people humbly sold out for the gospel.

Paul found people hungry to fulfill God's purposes, meet needs, and do something together beyond what they could even imagine through the power of God himself working in and amongst them.

I am reminded in Scripture of a prophet who came to a lady's house who had nothing left in her house but enough to feed her only son and then die. The prophet said, "God has sent me—use your last oil and make me a meal" (1 Kings 17:13). God was waiting to see her faith. And, when she did as instructed... well, you know the rest of the story. She never ran out. She kept pouring. He said He would *build His church and the gates of hell would not prevail against it*. He will build His church and He uses people like you and me to do it.

> *"Your needs are not about money. They're about faith. And, about people humbly sold out for the gospel."*

It would be a strange appeal. But remarkably they did give! And they gave liberally, freely, and with genuine concern and prayers. Have you considered how the Macedonian Christians donated? They gave in a manner that no one else knew what they had given, anonymously. They gave so abundantly it likely shocked far more than Paul. They gave generously. They gave without having to be coerced to do so, totally voluntarily. And, they gave individually and from a personal vantage point of commitment.

> *"Your people will see and experience in you how they should respond and serve. Sheep need a shepherd."*

> *"Let each one do just as he has purposed in his heart; not grudgingly or under compulsion; for God loves a cheerful giver."* 2 Corinthians 9:7 (NASB 1977)

And the Bible says in 1 Peter 5:2–3 that "we" as pastor/leaders should be the examples to the flock. It begins with us. Your people will see and experience in you how they should respond and serve. Sheep need a shepherd.

Genuine servanthood leads to authentic givers. If we are sincere bondservants of Christ, servants of the Lord, we are looking, listening, discerning, and walking in His presence to *find a hurt and heal it, to find a need and meet it* (the anthem of William Booth, founder of the Salvation Army). We're not called to walk by it— the hurts and pains of the world's cries. We're called to heal it. And, for the missions

> *"Somehow in finding the depth of our own brokenness we bring a salve and hope to others dealing with similar pains."*

context, when you see people who don't know Jesus—*Here am I, send me.* I can't be like Dr. Dimitrov or whomever you view with great humble esteem. He didn't call you to be him... He called you to be you. Be the best you that you can be. He's called us to share a hurt and share what He's done in your life. Somehow in finding the depth of our own brokenness we bring a salve and hope to others dealing with similar pains. Givers who need no recognition can give with no reservation. They'll give without reluctance and without selfish/self-centered restrictions. These types of leaders, these types of givers—these types of humble givers—are rare indeed. It takes self-denial. It takes commitment to follow through.

> "Let each one do just as he has purposed in his heart; not grudgingly or under compulsion; for God loves a cheerful giver." 2 Corinthians 9:7 (NASB)

> "He who is generous will be blessed." Proverbs 22:9 (NASB)

American pastor and author Charles Swindoll told a story:

> "In the mid-1940s, shortly after WWII came to a close, Europe began picking up the pieces. Much of the old country had been ravaged by war and was in ruins. And, there were thousands of young orphaned children starving on the streets of war-torn cities. Early one cold morning a gentleman of compassion was making his way back to his barracks in London. Turning the corner he spotted a little lad with his nose pressed to the window of a pastry shop. Inside, the cook was kneading dough for fresh bread and donuts. The hungry boy stared in silence watching every move of the baker. The gentleman pulled his jeep to the side of the road and

> *knelt down beside the child asking if he wanted
> some of that bread. The oven was steaming up the
> windows of the bakery and the boy was startled
> when the soldier asked this of him. 'YES. YES,' he
> said. The man went inside, purchased a dozen
> loaves of bread and donuts and brought the piping
> hot treats to the little boy, with a simple, 'here you
> go—this is for you.' As he turned to walk away, the
> little boy tugged his coat and quietly asked...
> 'Mister... are you God?'"*

We are never more like God than when we give. *God so loved the world that ... He gave...*

Let's take a further moment to delve into theological foundations of monetary giving and of the raising of missions support. I primarily want to address biblical giving, but I recognize I address these matters from my own lens. I can only speak from my own perspectives. And, as I've said before, perspective is reality to the people who have it. I was raised in a Baptist home with Baptist theology and Baptist church structure and polity when it came to the matters of giving and offerings for missions, above the tithe. When I joined the present denomination I serve, there was an entirely

> *"We are never more like God than when we give. God so loved the world that... He gave..."*

different, and still theologically based and well-developed, understanding of the same matters. For example, in most all Baptist congregations, the church as a whole would offer support to a denominationally approved missions ministry organization. It's a wonderful plan. Funds would be sent to that organization and that organization would then support the denomination's missionaries around the world. Individuals would give solely to and through their local church, to which the church would—usually as a whole and in a church-wide business meeting—determine such amounts. But, to me, there was a personal element that was missing. In the Assemblies of God, with the typical exception of the decisions of that nature being made by church-wide all-church business meetings, many of the churches likewise receive missions offerings provided by members. Those offerings are then sent to various individual missionaries the local church or her leadership has chosen to support. And, many individuals give directly to certain missionaries they believe the Lord has given them a personal heart or burden to pray for or assist in their respective ministries. These two approaches through the two separate denominational structures are simply a difference in the "how" of supporting missions and missionaries.

I shared earlier in this book the memory of a letter I had received from my very faithful Baptist father. Later in life he would show his love more freely and would tear up easily.

Still, in that letter he had also explained to me how he could not in good conscious support any *asking for support* that I had likely solicited for a missions trip of which I was about to travel. His reasons had to do with his perspective that if God had called me, the church I attended would support me, and God would provide through and only through His Church.

I wasn't broken or injured in any way from my father's words. But I, of course, did not forget them. They were a lifelong example to me to contextually recognize, "Who is the Church?" And, I determined, from my perspective and study of God's Word, the Church is not the organization, but solely those individuals, the actual people called by His name and faithful to follow, work, and serve Christ, alone. Thus, it appeared to me, it was a scripturally and theologically sound directive to allow

> *"They're asking for Jesus and for the endeavor of taking His message around the globe."*

individuals to support missional works or missionaries, or churches, or para-church ministries, or non-profits, or a myriad of social impacting charitable organizations if and when the child of God had prayerfully determined it was in God's encouragement to do so. Now years later, I remind missionaries (since that's our topic of this conversation) when they ask for financial support from a believer, a child of God (who actually is and makes up the true Church), they are not asking for themselves. They're asking for the work of the gospel. They're asking for Jesus and for the endeavor of taking His message around the globe. We spent ample time earlier with this point, but may we never forget, for the believer, they're either called to go or to send. Jesus said, *Go ye therefore...* There's no questioning whether or not it is God's will. And, if I can't go, then someone should ask if I could/would help send.

Let's talk about the overall theological implications of scriptural giving. Giving is an adventure in blessing. It's personal. From a pneumatic context (Holy Spirit directed), it changes the way you live. It becomes an intimate and beautiful challenge to living as a servant of God. Giving is an acknowledgement that God is owner of all. It's an evidence of faith and a Christian witness. I will go so far to say that giving is a biblical minimum...in tithes and in offerings above. One's giving to the things of God is a symbol of dedication and an expression of gratitude for all He's done for us.

> *"Giving is an adventure in blessing."*

Leviticus 27:32 teaches us that our tithe is holy unto the Lord. Now, the Bible is the same whether in Europe or in Africa, in India or in Peru. What it says for one in Ecuador, it says for one in Cameroon, China, Australia, or wherever one lives.

Proverbs 3:9–10 teaches us that one tithes from the gross, the total of what you make, not the net. It was from the first fruits. If you get a job, I believe the Bible says that whatever you make in salary, the first tenth of it belongs to God. All of it came from God and He asks us to tithe (a term meaning a tenth, a first fruits, from the very first of it).

That's quite a challenge here in Europe as your taxes are very high. But, I've always taught that the Bible says to honor God first and He'll take care of everything else.

> *"Proverbs 3:9–10 teaches us that one tithes from the gross, the total of what you make, not the net. It was from the first fruits."*

In the financing of *missio Dei*, we must be first—ourselves and individually—partakers of financial giving. The Bible says in Malachi 3:8–10 if we are not obedient, we will be robbing God. It tells us where we're to give our money; we are to bring tithes and offerings into the storehouse. And, it tells us that as we give, we will be blessed. First Chronicles 29:6–17 says God blessed Israel because they offered willingly. Second Chronicles 31 says the storehouse is your local church. And, James 1:17 says that every blessing comes from God. I personally believe that businesses and ministries should also tithe and give offerings to the work of the Lord (See Num. 18:24–28).

I don't make this stuff up. I didn't write it. I just read it. It's Bible. Many frown on giving or taking on the challenge of giving to the church or to God's work, especially amidst the challenges of their own family struggles or financial commitments. But, the Bible speaks for itself. My part is learning to walk in faith. I've found through the years, He is faithful. Some will say, "Sure, you've found it easy to tithe. Your wife is a physician." Sadly, we've had people make those kinds of remarks from time to time. But, what about the early years of our marriage, when she wasn't? Those were years where we lived on love, and enjoyed $0.25 (twenty-five cent) boxed meals from the grocery. Those were years when at times my all-commission sales job would not provide very much monthly income. I remember our commitment then to tithe faithfully throughout our entire married life, whether we had much or little. And, those weekly tithe checks we wrote were often less than $7. That's correct. Just a year or so ago, Renee was going through old files and found one of our first married-life tithe checks: $6 and change. We'd always write the tithe, to the penny, trying to make sure we didn't rob God in any way. And, we still made it, somehow. God provided.

> "The Bible speaks for itself. My part is learning to walk in faith."

You see, I'm convinced, provided someone had it, they wouldn't tithe on a million dollar income unless they had first learned the amazing faithfulness of God in their tithe on the $7 amount. God will prove himself strong. Trust Him. If you're reading this now and thinking to yourself, "How could we possibly give another 10 percent to God's work?" Just pray about it. I think as you talk it over with God, you and He will come to some understandings of His amazing grace and His amazing provision for you and your families. Maybe He's just waiting on us to see if we'll walk in faith.

So, as a young pastor of a smaller church that I desperately wanted to be a missional church, I had to come to early decisions about giving, both personally and corporately for our church itself. The people the Lord had given our congregation didn't give a lot of money for missions at first. The church we pastored—it

> *"Maybe He's just waiting on us to see if we'll walk in faith."*

was initially a challenging situation. When we first went there, I assumed the role as the worship leader for the services and we served as the youth pastors of a small—very small—group of 3 to 5 teenagers. I attended university on a partial music scholarship, so music was something I did for the church and it came comfortably and naturally, as I enjoyed serving alongside a few other key singers and musicians from the small church. After giving my life unreservedly to Christ, I had become a worshipper by nature and longed to worship and lead others into His presence.

I had in my heart, even as a youth pastor, that I wanted to raise up a missions-minded group of teenagers. I told our young people that they were going to raise $3,000 to give to missions. Now, in those days that was a lot of money. How? They sold cookies...and did everything imaginable. I finally decided they were not going to raise $3,000 by selling cookies, so I took two of the most influential of the five to my corner and humble office. Giving them an old-fashioned phone book (standard for the day), I told them to call everyone they knew explaining what they were doing, and that there were people who needed food, that there were churches that needed planting, and that there were people who needed to know Jesus. I told the two to simply end their brief and bold statement of faith with a simple "ask" for a one-time gift of $10 or more.

It took hours. But, during an all-night fun event with the few others and some friends who had attended, the two teenagers worked the phones, called family members, teachers, friends, and random strangers. Believe it not, they raised enough to add to "the cookie funds," and by the end of that first year our small and fledgling youth group was named the #1 missions supporting youth group in the Assemblies of God in the state. I can still see in my mind's eye the pride and excitement those few young people experienced when they were awarded what came as such a high honor. From the entire state and from their feeling no one knew they even existed or that anything they could ever do would actually make much of a difference for the kingdom of God, they shined a bright light for Jesus and made a difference for missions and missionaries all around the world.

It's not about money. It's about relationship. Through the years, I've often gotten on the phone or spoken to someone in person and simply asked, "Would you be willing to help us? This is what we're trying to do. It's something that we've not done before. Would you give a one-time gift of $X to help us?" Almost every time, I encounter people who say, "Yes." I've found God's people are the most generous and giving people in the world.

> *"I've found God's people are the most generous and giving people in the world."*

You have not, because you ask not. How should you give? Second Corinthians 8:2–5 tells us the people gave liberally, but first they gave themselves to the Lord: holiness, sanctification, and consecration. When people give, 1 Chronicles 29:14 teaches we give to God what is already His. It's all God's anyway. You and I—or the people you're asking of—are only stewards (the keepers) of what God has entrusted to us or them.

Then, in 2 Corinthians 9:6–8, we learn of the law of sowing and reaping. You will reap more than you sow. God's returns are in multiple form. The missionary appeal of asking for money is not about the needs. It's about Jesus. Every time you ask someone to help the gospel, they don't know it, but you're blessing them.

Every Christian today is the product of the missionary work of yesterday. Heaven is our destination. And, billions around the world still do not know His name or have this hope.

> *"Every time you ask someone to help the gospel, they don't know it, but you're blessing them."*

- Will you go?
- Will you accept the call?
- Will you send someone accepting the call to go?
- Will you challenge me to give so that you might go?

Each servant of God is a steward of possessions for which God has entrusted into their care. What possessions are to be considered? How about these? When you have time, take the extra moments to study God's Word and the Scripture references provided to see what the Bible actually says about each topic:

- Our Money (Luke 21:1–4)
- Our Time (Eph. 2:10, 5:15–17)

- Our Items Owned (Matt. 19:16–23)
- Our Bodies (1 Cor. 6:19)
- Our Families (1 Tim. 3:4–5, 5:4)
- Our Ministries (1 Pet. 4:10)

The Bible also offers detailed answers to our questions about stewardship, giving, and money. The theology of stewardship and the financing of missions (taking His life and gospel message to the ends of the earth) is a fabulous study. Take these Scriptures into account as you consider your own life and any tweaks you might sense Him drawing you toward:

- Leviticus 27:30–32; Malachi 3:8–12 (Tithing in the OT Law)
- Exodus 25:1–8 (The Free-will Offering for the Tabernacle)
- 1 Chron. 29:1–20 (David Models Giving for the Building of the Temple)
- Luke 21:1–4 (Giving Out of Poverty)
- 1 Cor. 9:4–14; 1 Tim. 5:18 (The Financing of NT Church Leaders)
- 1 Cor. 16:1–2, 2 Cor. 8:1–6 (The Collection for the Jerusalem Saints)

Beyond each of these passages, there are clear and distinguishable principles of personal giving of finances in the Bible. Every believer should give. Our giving should be in proportion to our income, both cash and non-cash. Imagine if God made your income proportional to what you are now giving. And, we're also to give, even in our poverty. Maybe you are giving, and giving much, to family, friends, or good projects. But, are you giving to the work of the Lord, scripturally? That's what really matters. It's not what I think is "enough", or what I believe is "good enough". What matters is what the Bible actually says; what God's Word actually teaches. John 1 teaches us, the Word has been from the beginning. It was and is…God. And, He became flesh in Jesus and lived his amazing life before us and for us, that we might know Him and the power of this touch and healing for all mankind.

We are to give with generosity and because we desire to give not because someone forces us. Remember, your giving must be from a willing heart in order to please God. We are to give more than we are able (trusting God). That's called faith. Further, our financial giving should follow the giving of ourselves to God. Giving is a demonstration of devotion to the Lord.

> "What matters is what the Bible actually says; what God's Word actually teaches."

So, every believer should give. First, tithe. First, give tithe unto the Lord. Start there. Once you are faithful there, the

Bible teaches—seemingly always stretching me to grow deeper and stronger in faith and in my trust of His faithfulness—to go beyond the tithe and give offerings above. Every believer should give. Challenge yourself with how faithful you've been to giving. Sure, you give to the local schools or to local young people in their sports endeavors or fruit sales at holidays. But, have you considered giving to God? Am I genuinely living out faith? Am I a biblical servant? Am I a giver? It starts there.

Now, obedience is why we do missions.

> *"All authority in heaven and on earth has been given to me. Therefore go and make disciples of all nations, baptizing them in the name of the Father, and of the Son, and of the Holy Spirit, and teaching them to obey everything I have commanded you. And surely I am with you always, to the very end of the age."* Matthew 28:18–20 (NIV)

We cannot afford to lose sight of the plan that God has given us. The battles of the church are not won on the football field, but in prayer. The strongholds of the enemy are not torn down in the fellowship hall, but torn down in the prayer hall. In Acts 4:31, the Bible tells us that *"when they had prayed, the place was shaken"* (KJV). So your financing the things of God begins there.

Here in Brussels, I've passed out:

- A gift of a Bible bookmarker—to pray for Renee and me after we leave.
- A gift of a Faith Promise giving brochure to explain further how Assemblies of God missionaries are funded by local congregations and individuals. And,
- A gift of a practical example of how to raise funds for missions, from something I've personally done recently.

Let's turn our attention to specifically speaking about the raising of personal support (if you're a missionary) through what the Assemblies of God (my own fellowship) would call Faith Promise commitments. The AG standard protocol in the West, not likely as so in Europe, Africa, the Islands, or the East, can be for some daunting and intimidating, challenging even, at best. But, it is theologically sound and biblically implicated for both the worker (the goer) raising support and (the sender), the individual or the church who accepts the missional mandate.

I've lived it, and I'm a first-hand witness to the enormous blessings for churches and individuals that are missions supporting churches!

*"Depend on it. God's work done in God's way will never lack God's supply. He is too wise a God to frustrate His purposes for lack of funds, and He can just as easily supply them ahead of time as afterwards, and He much prefers doing so."* James Hudson Taylor

97

Regretfully, most pastors or church missions committees need to reassess their budgetary process. It is not uncommon for them to sense their core priority is to define a missions budget and resolve how to implement or spend it. I propose, rather, the Spirit-led missions pastor or committee will understand everything the church does as a fulfillment of *missio Dei* (the mission of God) encounters and ministries. The all-inclusive church or ministry budget is a missional account for God's intended purpose of "Go ye therefore..."

> *"Regretfully, most pastors or church missions committees need to reassess their budgetary process."*

To do this, we should consider first how God is at work. Then, we can determine how we are to work with Him. Find out what God is doing and what God is blessing. Therein spend your time, build your church, and expend all your efforts and resources.

- Where do I see God at work?
- Where and how is God working in the lives of those around me?
- Where and how is God working in my neighborhood?
- In light of my gifts and resources, how does God want me to partner with Him in what He is doing?

If you are a pastor or going to be a pastor/leader of a church, you need to track church finances with accountability and with careful record keeping. One person must never be placed in charge. Have two or more individuals to receive, count, log, and deposit church funds. And, we don't do anything behind closed doors. Be transparent with the church. Those are simple and expected protocols of integrity and accountability.

If you ask someone for $10, you should with reliability return to them and explain exactly what you did with their $10. This is important because you/I plan on coming back to that person again. Why will I ask them again? The answer seems obvious, or maybe it doesn't to some. I will ask again because I found in them a heart that was willing to invest in the gospel. Next time, I will ask for $100 dollars. But only after I've prayed. Only after I know I'm walking in the Holy Spirit's directive. I will return and again ask—only after I've looked into the person's eyes and heart—whether they are a believer or not. You can see if they are a good person who wants to do good. "May I help you to do good?" should be our perspective. "Can we partner together to do good?"

> *"Find out what God is doing and what God is blessing. Therein spend your time, build your church, and expend all your efforts and resources."*

99

Just be the best you that you can be, and let some of Jesus rub off on whomever you are with. Many times—for $100—the people you're sharing with will say, "Yes."

I've raised a lot of money for missions through the years. Not once have I ever raised anything for "me." As we spoke earlier, remember that you don't raise it for you—it's all about Him.

Let's focus a moment on the overall finances of the church. As we think about the basics of managing church finances, there are some standard items to be addressed. First, teach systematic giving. Develop a budget and accurately track income and expenses. Train the church treasurer and other members responsible for church finances. You can never train too much. In my experience, most of those (like myself) called to pastor are adept at sharing God's Word but not so skilled or learned in financial accounting or bookkeeping. Certainly, that was the case for me. I'm grateful the Lord has given me a wonderful team through the years to help our church systems be healthy, strong, and accountable.

Keep in mind that a system for collecting and distributing funds should include several people, prayerful planning, accountability, regular collecting, careful record keeping, and regular reporting. Again, one person must not have total control. And, be transparent with the church about financial matters. Give regular reports to the church as needed. There are churches that have annual business meetings as well as protocols for any member to ask questions or to receive a full accounting of the finances. There are other churches whose structure may be more like a Baptist church, with monthly all-church meetings. However your church functions, do it with integrity and humble accountability.

Now, certainly, (and I'll capitalize this for emphasis) CHURCHES AND INDIVIDUALS ARE TO SUPPORT MISSIONS. Let's talk for just a few moments about part of my own story. Everybody has a story. Here's some of mine.

When we took a pastorate some years ago, we'd been previously the youth pastors for about four years. At the time we became pastors our church had no building. We were renting a school. The pastor I previously worked for, who was a dear and trusted friend, had just entered proceedings to divorce his wife. It was a challenging

> "However your church functions, do it with integrity and humble accountability."

time for us all. We had lost a lot of people, and it was a trial. The church board at the time, after a several month search for a pastor that didn't seem to be so fruitful, said to me, "You seem to love your wife." They actually said that.

(Laughter). "And, you've been with us for four years. It seems also few others want to come or seem right to us—to be here. Would you be willing to stay and help us?" Elwood Puckett and Jack Aldridge were wonderful, faithful, called, and most genuine friends and leaders. Renee and I will never forget them.

We loved the people and we loved the church. Furthermore, we had come to the church and accepted the staff position four years earlier only after three (not one, not two, but three) confirmations from completely different people and in completely different occasions had given us a clear direction of the Lord's leading. So, we firmly believed we were still in the center of His will, regardless of the disconcerting moments we'd been facing in the church of recent. And, we said, "Yes."

That first year of our pastorate, the church with many continued challenges—stabilizing to attendance of just fewer than 100 people—gave about $15,000 to missions. I applauded them for their giving, in the middle of their hurt—hurt by their pastor, often weeping, and with many of their families having left the church. A small core hung in there. But, I knew in my heart of hearts that $15,000 was not enough to please me, their new pastor, nor was it an amount that I felt was "the best the church could do" for the Lord's work. So we began to challenge them.

We gave to every missionary we could afford to give to. Then, somehow I started to think like the world. I started to expect and accept, as would the world. "We only have so much money, Pastor. We can only support so many, Pastor. You know the roof is leaking, Pastor..."

Then, we had a missionary couple visit our church, Steve and Deanne Turley. They said they were called to Brussels. He may remember better than do I, as he's sitting in today's audience, but I definitely remember saying, "No." I had given to every missionary I could give to and we simply had no more money. There were even conversations from time to time as to which bills would be paid and at what point the salaries of the staff and myself would be cut. The Lord had been blessing our church, but the challenges were all I could see. The Lord had helped us with property—nearly 40 acres. And, we had built the first building—a simple construction— an open rectangular room of 3,000 square feet, one small and nearly perfectly square room for a nursery, and small restrooms. That was it. It was wall to wall seats and a small platform inside with only (I think) a 12-foot ceiling (which I had pushed for in our initial build, because the simple and low-cost efficiency of that first phase of building plans had listed it at only 8-foot ceiling heights. I cringed at that thought so, was grateful to have the extended ceilings, if only 12 feet high. It was humble, but it housed our people.

"Steve, I have no more money, but I'll pray for you." And,

without blinking, as I remember it, he responded, "You have said you want to build a great missions church. You can't afford not to give to me. It's not about what you have in your account. It's about whether you have the faith to bring in what you don't have." It pierced me like a sword. I knew I had no money, but I think I gave him a $50 monthly pledge, and told him, "Steve, if it comes in, I'll give it."

Over the next year as I instructed the bookkeeper to pay all our missionaries first, and me last, not one month came that the money was not provided and we were not able to fulfill our promise to Steve Turley, along with the other missionaries we were already supporting. And, not one time that year did I not get paid, as well. God was faithful. Over the years, we increased that pledge—doubled it—and, though I am almost fifteen years past having been the pastor, to this day that church still supports the missionary endeavors of Steve and Deanne Turley in Brussels and throughout Europe.

> *"You have said you want to build a great missions church. You can't afford not to give to me."*

On our ten-year anniversary as the pastors the Lord blessed us to dedicate the nearly 40 acres of land and an approximately $2 million facility. A childcare facility with an early edge toward academics (King's Way Academy) was in operation with 150 children five days per week. And, staff of over 25 employees worked as a team (for the most part) to run the childcare academy and the church. Two years later, on our twelve-year anniversary as pastors, the church had 400 people in regular attendance, and 500 to 650 people on Christmas and Easter gave $430,000 to missions, a per capita giving of over $1,000 per person in the church. To put that in perspective, I recently heard for the USA, the Southern Baptists per capita giving last year (2017) was about $30 per person. The Assemblies of God per capita giving last year (2017) was about $80 per person. That year (2004), after only twelve years of MISSIONAL PNEUMATOLOGY, that church gave over $1,000 per capita (per person). Now, keep in mind the roughly 400 people included about 100 children, which meant the approximately 300

> *"That year (2004), after only twelve years of MISSIONAL PNEUMATOLOGY, that church gave over $1,000 per capita (per person)."*

regularly attending adults in the congregation gave $430,000 to missions over and above their tithe (which is what kept the ministry sites operational). It was a remarkable twelve-year journey that began with approximately $15,000 in missions giving. It was significant and extraordinary.

But look what happened. As I just explained, on the TEN YEAR ANNIVERSARY the church was dedicating their owned nearly 40 acres and approximately $2 million in facilities on the land, which included the new facility, the property, and a large 5,000-square-foot homestead that had served a myriad of ministry purposes—offices, children's ministries, fellowship hall, and kitchen facilities—and ultimately became a home for unwed mothers led by a faithful couple in our church.

Another ½ acre of land and a newly built facility housed the large childcare ministry a few miles away in the small community. That facility was another $ ½ million of assets.

We were on staff at the church for sixteen years, previously serving four years as youth pastor, worship / music director, and associate pastor. Then, what I would often call the journey of the "King's Way Miracle" began.

The Bible works whether in the US, Florida, Ghana, Italy, or Belgium. You get my point. The Bible is the same yesterday, today, and forever. I have come to recognize miracle stories of this nature do not occur in every situation. There are countless faithful and spiritually godly leaders who never see such growth as quickly. But, I also know His faithfulness is sure and true in each and every body of believers doing what He so desires in those ministries, as well. So how does this relate to missions? Completely. Directly. Utterly. Wholly. I am now totally convinced, as I've lived it, that when God's people focus on the things important to Jesus, He takes care of every other matter in our lives. For a church to be, in my opinion, a genuinely Bible-faithful church and a church that wholly follows Jesus, there is no question that they'll give faithfully to missions and missionaries. Why do I believe in missions? It makes good sense...

Renee and I were young and in our first pastorate. We followed a wonderful friend as pastor, yet a friend/pastor who had his challenges—personally, spiritually, emotionally during that particular time in his life. Gratefully, he later found his way and re-entered the ministry, but his days at this church were completed and the damages rendered could not be undone. Ultimately, the church became divided, downtrodden, and burdened. The leaders and membership had lost their way, becoming nearly helpless and hopeless. There's a lot more that could be expounded, but let's suffice to say, at those moments of uncertainty, God was still on the throne and had a plan. The Bible says, His plans for us are good, with a future and a hope (Jer. 29:11). And, He had plans to bring about His healing in both the lives of the broken pastor and the families involved with those matters, as well as for His beloved Church.

> *"I am now totally convinced, as I've lived it, that when God's people focus on the things important to Jesus, He takes care of every other matter in our lives."*

YEAR TWELVE of our pastorate found Renee and me being elected by Assemblies of God ministers to serve the AG USA as district superintendent for the state of Kentucky. Other denominations might call the position "State Bishop." It was a humbling season, elected as the youngest district superintendent for the Assemblies of God in America at the time, at only 41 years of age when colleagues of the same across the nation were characteristically in their 50s, 60s, and 70s. The "youngest status" only lasted weeks to months, as another young first-time district superintendent by the name of Doug Clay was elected in nearby Ohio. It was a time filled with anticipation, dreams, and the "almost immediate" weight of the mantle.

All that occurred? How does that happen? I've been asked many times, "What was your secret?" There was no secret. There was only a secret place.

> *"I've been asked many times, "What was your secret?" There was no secret. There was only a secret place."*

Why do I believe in missions? It makes good sense. Let's take a moment to look at a few points that I'd like to draw to your attention.

Take your sickle and reap... (Rev. 14:14–16, NIV)

1. I've heard it said churches that have missions

conventions report up to 67 percent more salvations. Though I don't know exactly where that statistic would have originated, let's say the number is only 50 percent. Who wouldn't want to focus on missions if they were called to pastor a church?! Beyond that, those churches raise more missions money. And, their own churches, statistically, bring in more money in tithes and offerings for the church's general fund accounting.

> *"I've heard it said churches that have missions conventions report up to 67 percent more salvations."*

Missions dollars are not tithes. When I asked members or parishioners for $10 for missions (or whatever amount), at least after an earlier season of training the people for our purposes, I became quite confident the giver did not take that out of their tithes. In the USA we spend more money on cell phones, on dog food, on movies and entertainment, far more on restaurants and meals... than missions. In the US, a cell phone will cost about $600 or more and everybody has one. Fathom it. In the US we spend more on pets than missions. I challenge you— financing the mission of God is personal. Look into your life on a practical basis

> *"Missions dollars are not tithes."*

and find out how much you spend on frivolous things.

How much could you actually be financing the mission of God?

Coffee was something I never drank in college. Only until the maturity of grey hair and expanded waistlines did I acquire the taste. Starbucks coffee shops became synonymous with vogue and living a life that made one feel they were relevant and hip. At least, to my generation, that seems to be a good analogy. Admittedly, those who know me know a Starbucks gift card is a safe gift, as I patron every Starbucks I see, from my hometown to the cities and travel destinations on my schedule across the globe. A few years ago, I had a conversation with a cousin as we laughed about the amount of money we had inadvertently spent at Starbucks coffee-shops over the past year. To this day, I remember the angst I felt, as a moment of guilt and reality struck me, as to the number of souls and lives I could have impacted with the gospel with those dollars spent on coffee.

If we lived in a different context, you might be from a very wealthy family, but you don't have to walk in "wealth" ... Wealth is not wrong. Go with me for just a moment to understand what I'm speaking of here. He blesses a cheerful giver. And the Bible says even the wicked will prosper. But, His eyes are roaming to and fro throughout the whole earth looking for hearts turned toward him so he can bless them. (2 Chronicles 16:9).

If you have been privileged, receive it as a crown and bless the Kingdom. Trust me. You really did not accomplish it on your own. *Every good and perfect gift is from above.* If like me you were raised in humble surroundings, wear it like a crown and walk in the—"more"—of a faithful God! Because He blesses a cheerful giver, when they are Kingdom-minded.

> *"If you have been privileged, receive it as a crown and bless the Kingdom."*

2. I believe in missions because It's Simply Biblical.

2 Peter 3:9—*THE FATHER is not willing that anyone should perish...*
Luke 19:10—*THE SON came to seek and save that which was lost...*
And, John 16:8—*THE HOLY SPIRIT came to convict the world of sin and draw all men to Christ.*

Why Do I Believe in Missions?

1. Because I believe:
   - *Anyone who calls upon the name of the Lord will be saved.*

111

- *But how, they ask. How can they believe? ...if they have never heard.*
- *Unless someone tells them...and unless someone is sent.* (Rom. 10:13–15)

2. On the personal side, I knew it was a personal call—for me and for every follower of Christ—"Go ye therefore..." As a Pastor, I knew I was the key. As I led, they would follow. Sheep need a shepherd. Sheep follow. Shepherds lead.

I knew missions would make my church successful. And what pastor doesn't want their church to be favored and successful? And, I know...

> *"Salvation is found in no one else, for there is no other name under heaven given to mankind by which we must be saved."* Acts 4:12 (NIV)

When you choose to get involved, you can't help but respond, because time is running out. Jesus said,

> *"All of us must quickly carry out the tasks assigned us by the one who sent me, for there is little time left before the night falls and all the work comes to an end."* John 9:4 (TLB)

So, I got involved personally.

I believe there are some today—hearing this, reading this—whom God has called to be missionaries. Do not be afraid to ask for support. You're not asking for yourself. You're asking for Jesus. It's biblical. It's theologically sound. Blame it on the apostle Paul, who asked of Macedonia, and recognize the poor might give more than the wealthy.

Never be afraid to go to a small church, a small home group, a small event. All it takes is one elderly lady who hears your heart—and God's—and while no one else gives, she pulls out her checkbook and blesses the work of the Lord from the intimacy of her heart.

> *"As a Pastor, I knew I was the key. As I led, they would follow. Sheep need a shepherd. Sheep follow. Shepherds lead."*

Maybe it will be for you like it was in my church when I pastored, when the elderly woman who no one thought had much money at all wrote a large check. Some even asked me, privately, *"Do you think this is real?"* I said, *"Take it to the bank and find out."* It was real. Or, like the anonymous person (likely a lady) in our church that when a missions offering was taken, simply dropped in the offering plate a diamond ring. Or maybe it will be like the family that raised horses (our church was situated in beautiful

> *"He's looking for a heart turned toward Him."*

Kentucky race horse country) and said they felt led to breed, deliver, raise, and sell a horse—for missions. Or, like the church visitor who came to church one time—and on that one day—a missions offering was being received and he wrote a check for $8,000. Those are all true examples of God using regular people to do extraordinary things for the work of Christ around the world.

Or, maybe it will be like the young college student, when the missionary came and the student didn't have anything to give, simply wrote on a small scrap sheet of paper, *"My offering is—I give you my life..."* dropping it in the offering plate as it passed by. And today, I am the most blessed man in the world, because He's looking for a heart turned toward Him. Unfaithful and broken in so many ways, as we all are, I do yearn to honor the Lord Who has so blessed my life. In your own journey, remember, it's not about you. It's all about Jesus.

Would you give for the needs of someone you do not know? To put shoes on feet, bread on tables, help young people and children to go to school, to have clothes and a Bible? If you are one who would say, "Yes," then in the system I'm accustomed, place your name and check a box to simply say to the Lord, "I'll give on faith monthly, weekly, or however. But, I'll give for You, Lord."

At the beginning of every month, write the tithe before

you pay your rent, before you buy your dog food... not so you'll be blessed...but because you know He is the One who blesses a cheerful giver. Then, write your missions check— Faith Promise giving. It's not what you own or money you think you can afford. It's what you trust Him for. When people begin to live in that level of faith, the miraculous, the apostolic, the prophetic, the uncommon, and the supernatural occur in ways you'll never be able to

> *"Stepping to the platform, I was moved to tears in His presence—awaiting, standing, waiting in His presence."*

explain. For some, those situations in your families or for your extended family members that cripple you in hurt and in prayers will amazingly take a turn for healing and health. For others, years of waiting to see a prayer answered may include years more—until that beautiful day of God's touch. But, it will come. I'm convinced. It will come.

MISSIONS INVOLVES:
GOERS
SENDERS
WHICH ARE YOU?

Stepping to the platform, I was moved to tears in His presence—awaiting, standing, waiting in His presence...a holy hush came upon the audience in Brussels. The interpreter quietly whispering, sensitively, her own in-the-

115

Spirit prayers in French. Then, after a deep breath, I spoke...

The problem with the world today is...they are not challenged. The problem with the Church today is...His amazing grace has stopped being amazing. May we be broken for the world. And, may His amazing grace on your life be transferred to everyone you see and touch. For those who have children, may His anointing be richer on them than it is on you. Richer on our children that it is on us.

## Section Four

### Cultural Contextualization

We have spoken about redemptive contextualization. We have spoken about missional pneumatology. We have spoken about financial contextualization. Today, we're going to speak about cultural contextualization.

But before I begin, I feel led to move in a different direction. I asked permission of Silvia and Tia (both names changed for publication purposes)—two of your own—if they would join me on the platform.

*Silvia*: I came from London; London, England. God put me in positions which I could have never imagined to be without a university degree. I know what it is like to have money in a bank account, so when God asked me to come to

Belgium, I left everything not knowing what I would find here. But, I wanted to live as the Bible says we can live. So, I did not know even how to say, "Hello." My life completely changed. I went to work in a cottage taking care of two babies, but God was teaching me how to trust Him and depend only upon Him, not on my bank account, my job, or my own hands.

> *"God was teaching me how to trust Him and depend only upon Him."*

God directed me to come to CTS. I was planning to start my career again in Belgium in business, but I had to change everything again. And it's very hard. I had to work to pay for my studies, my house, and to help my mom with some medicines back in Brazil. So lately I got to a point where it's been really hard to manage it all by myself. People have said that I'm crazy. "What are you doing? How are you going to make money in the future?" But, I know I have made the best decision in coming here and for what God wants for my life.

My point is, Dr. Joe was talking about tithes and offerings yesterday. Since I came to Belgium... I really learned and applied this in my life. Even though I don't earn much money, I don't know how, but I have everything that I need and I even bless people when I can. So, this last month I was praying, "God, I need a miracle to pay my school. If I could only have a miracle to pay for the end of the school year, I could breathe a little bit." Last Sunday, I stayed in my bedroom for hours and felt an assurance that God was really doing something. I wasn't afraid of anything. I said, "God, I know You're going to do something." I came to school on Monday, happy as usual, because I am very grateful to be here. And, I received news that a couple is willing to support me and had decided to pay my school bill for the entire semester. They said the Lord has touched their hearts. I knew God knows what I need, but He had already touched this couple to help me. While I was on my knees and talking to Him in intimacy, they did it. Although my bank account is red and I still have no money, my heart is full and to the point that I cannot explain. My school bills are paid! This is just the beginning. This is the encouragement of the size of my God. Some are here and not even your parents understand. Many people are against me saying I'm crazy with the job offers I had. But I prayed. I know in time people will see what God has done and how He's also called you. Just be obedient. The best is yet to come.

> "While I was on my knees and talking to Him in intimacy, they did it."

*Pastor Joe*: And so she came yesterday and said about tithing—once with much, now with little—but she gave anyway to be obedient, knowing she could not pay her school bill, knowing she would not have anything left, simply trusting that God would hear her heart. My

Redeemer is faithful and true.

*Silvia*: I give my tithing every month. The last two months to give tithe I had to take from my school money. And last month in church, even this occurred. I felt the Lord say to give everything I had in my wallet, then, for missions. I did it. I knew, how would I pay for school? Then, two weeks later, all this happened! Be faithful.

*Tia*: Hello everybody. I would like to tell you some of my testimony. I was converted when I was eighteen years old through a camp in our church. But I am a Christian today thanks to Students for Christ (SFC). I learned that young people could be passionate for Jesus and that I could be a leader. And, I learned that women could serve

> *"Because they were obedient to God's call to come here to serve students, my life changed."*

and even be pastors. I also learned that young people could go on mission for a year, a week, or for all their life. SFC has changed my life. Yesterday they spoke about tithes and offerings. SFC began with missionaries like Steve and Deanne Turley. Because they were obedient to God's call to come here to serve students, my life changed. And because they dared to ask for money—and churches gave—my life was changed. Lots of people who have passed through SFC have been completely transformed.

I think about four years ago I went on a camp for SFC and there was a Belgian there now in college, another who had done YWAM (Youth With A Mission), and another who had left on mission. There were three who continued to serve SFC after they finished their studies. (Two of them got married...) SFC has changed the lives of many because some said, "YES." So, yesterday when we were speaking about tithes and offerings it really touched me. Who cries when we speak about tithes and offerings? I did. God really spoke to me. It's a year and a half that I have been given to raise support for my mission call. Thinking about Steve and Deanne Turley, I know I will be a missionary.

But the last few months I've realized if I don't raise my support it's because I'm so proud. I find it difficult to ask people. I hate having to raise funds. It gives me a lot of stress, but I have to think about it because I have to pay also for the school and for the bus that brings me here every morning. What touched me yesterday was that it has less to do with us, but all to do with Jesus. My life was changed by Steve and Deanne's lives. I, too, would like to change lives now and in the future. Lives will be changed because I say "Yes" today. Sometimes we ask questions such as, "Are we going to live, have money, have support?" But God blesses and we just have to say "YES." When the day comes (the 15th for me at the school) that we have to send our money to pay for our tuition, I've learned it's nothing for God. We have to learn to trust Him. So, I encourage you all to say

121

"YES" to whatever God calls you to do with your life. Even if you have pride. Drop it. It's not to do with you. It's all about the lives to be changed because of you. Amen.

*Pastor Joe*: And...so she came yesterday...and it hit me. It matters. We've known this our whole lives. Until someone looks at you (and, I know this is not my home, but I feel like it's home) and she says, "Because you were willing to give to Steve and Deanne, I got saved." You can't afford not to give. Start now. Give now. Don't send it all back home (for those who carry the weight of families nations removed).

> *"Missions is not a program. It's the very heartbeat of God.*
> *(Dr. Beth Grant)."*

> *"Missions is not a program. It's the very heartbeat of God."* Dr. Beth Grant.

# The Cultural Contextualization of *Missio Dei*: "The Practical in Sharing Your Story and Reaching the Lost"

## 50 Missional Lessons Learned in 30+ Years of Ministry

Before you panic, let's stay connected to what God wants to say to us today. The mission of God is to reconcile relationships, heal brokenness, and bring wholeness in Christ and a flourishing to all who will receive it, to all who will follow.

"50 Missional Lessons" explores the multiplicity of ways in which we partner with God to bring about the fulfillment of God's desires for the world. God's mission is expressed in the redemptive and reconciling work of Christ, in the sanctifying and reconciling work of Jesus...in the narratives of Scripture and the Spirit's creation and ongoing re-creation of life for the people of God.

I just heard two testimonies of the recreation of life, and I can assure you when He touched my heart, He also changed my life. The lessons learned that we'll look at now involve one in analysis, affirmation, and pneumatalogical inspiration—the Spirit's inspiration—in light of the Church's historical, contemporary, and imminent sharing in God's mission. So, how does one actually reach people for Christ and move people for Christo-centric purpose? By further confronting Christian leaders to reexamine the good news in light of personal missional and ministry contexts.

Let's begin with a look at an abbreviated 7 Key Principles (from the overall 50 Missional Lessons).

For these particular seven, I went to a children's pastor. Not a professor, not a lead pastor, not an academic, but a children's pastor because to me they are a pastor. I gave him my 50 points and asked for him to simply return to me the seven he liked the best. So, I start with these seven for my new family here in Brussels.

## Key #1. (Lesson 17) Do more listening and observing than posturing.

Cultural contextualization. How do I win someone for Christ? Do more listening than talking and more observing than posturing. The world is filled with people looking for position. The world is filled with people looking to place themselves in positions. Do more listening and observing than posturing. When you listen you hear stories, you hear lives, you hear hurts, burdens, and all of a sudden putting and positioning yourself in a leadership role no longer matters. It's all about cultural contextualization. It's all about context. It becomes clear that the most important things in our lives around us are the beautiful relationships and the people we get to encounter along the way.

Scripture is all about context. It's all about seeing the lost saved. While I do not know what is in one man's heart, if I'll quit being whoever I think I am and simply be his friend, I will hear him. I will observe the beauty, and I will have the opportunity to reach his/their world for Christ. The Bible tells us about...

> *"Do more listening than talking and more observing than posturing."*

LISTENING

> *"...and he said, 'Listen, all Judah and the inhabitants of Jerusalem and King Jehoshaphat: thus says the LORD to you, 'Do not fear or be dismayed because of this great multitude, for the battle is not yours but God's.'"* 2 Chronicles 20:15 (NASB)

We need more willing people to listen. And we need more people willing to listen to the Lord that they might have a word from the Lord. People who can say assuredly, "Thus saith the word of the Lord." So we're told...all of Judah listen...

> *"Paul stood up, and motioning with his hand said, "Men of Israel, and you who fear God, listen:"* Acts 13:16 (NASB)

May we have more listening than posturing. This is meant to be practical: talk less and listen more.

Noted American author Helen Keller was a lecturer in the USA in the 1950s. She was the first deaf and blind woman in the United States to earn her bachelor's degree. Upon being asked, "What is the greatest tragedy?" She responded, "To have eyes, and not see." All of us are handicapped. She was blind. She was deaf. And she changed the world. All of us have handicaps. And it was the prophet Isaiah who said, *"Woe is me. I am undone..."* Isiah 6:5 (KJV). The most handicapped of all, he said he was. Maybe some of us need a few more physical handicaps so we can see.

> *"What is the greatest tragedy?' She responded, 'To have eyes, and not see.'"*

Do more listening and observing than posturing.

OBSERVING

> *"The LORD gives sight to the blind."* Psalm 146:8 (NIV)

> *"Now then, stand still and see this great thing the LORD is about to do before your eyes!"* 1 Samuel 12:16 (NIV)

*"Open my eyes that I may see wonderful things in Your law."* Psalm 119:18 (NIV)

AVOID POSTURING

The Bible also addresses how we should humble ourselves in the journey, drive, and push for status:

*"For everyone who exalts himself will be humbled, and he who humbles himself will be exalted."* Luke 14:11 (ESV)

**Key #2 (Lesson 25) There is no substitute for good communication.**

*"Let your speech always be gracious, seasoned with salt, so that you may know how you ought to answer each person."* Colossians 4:6 (ESV)

Your knowledge will not save any life bound by sin or separated from the love of Christ, but your heart for those and your heart for the Lord can change their lives forever. There is no substitute for good communication.

Our society has become obsessed with speaking positively. And, most are afraid to speak truthfully. So cultural contextualization instills in us to listen, observe, and speak with grace. It molds us to speak only that which needs to be spoken to any given person you're sharing with.

Why? Because, what I speak to that person might be culturally irrelevant or out of context for "that" person. What am I trying to say here? Pneumatological missiology, by its very nature, brings the hope that we may be filled with the presence of a holy God, so that I/we might know what to say to an individual...to a brother...to a king...to royalty...a president...or to the simplest of lives.

> *"Know this, my beloved brothers: let every person be quick to hear, slow to speak, slow to anger."* James 1:19 (ESV)

> *"A word fitly spoken [in season] is like apples of gold in a setting of silver."* Proverbs 25:11 (ESV)

> *"Let no corrupting talk come out of your mouths, but only such as is good for building up, as fits the occasion, that it may give grace [if I could add—in that occasion] to those who hear."* Ephesians 4:29 (ESV)

### Key #3 (Lesson 29) Unity has to be developed and then guarded at all costs.

Remember our topic: Cultural contextualization. There is power in unity. There is power in prayer. *Where one is they will put a thousand to flight. Where two are there they will put ten thousand to flight* (Deut. 32:30). Might we have two hundred and change a continent. Unity must be developed.

*"I appeal to you, brothers, by the name of our Lord Jesus Christ, that all of you agree, and that there be no divisions among you, but that you be united in the same mind and the same judgment."*
1 Corinthians 1:10, (ESV)

*"And above all these put on love, which binds everything together in perfect harmony."*
Colossians 3:14 (ESV)

Unity is created when people care about their team and care about their teammates. It's developed when they care about their team's goals. There are no lone rangers in the army of God. All of us are a part of a family of God and the Bible says to *put on love which binds everything together in harmony.*

> *"Pneumatological missiology, by its very nature, brings the hope that we may be filled with the presence of a holy God."*

My grandfather was a master stonemason. I can drive through one particular small town in Kentucky today and still see his handiwork. I do on occasions make that drive, finding serenity somehow with the simple glance as I drive by. When you're building a team, realize you can't build with someone who is not willing to help you carry bricks. So, when you see someone carrying the bricks, drop what you're doing and help them carry them. Why? Because it matters when it comes to saving the lost. They don't care how many degrees you have hanging on your walls. Common in Europe, I meet individuals with multiple degrees. But, when you meet the girl on the street who needs your help or you meet the young man, or the drug addict downtown, they do not care how many languages you speak. They want to know if you can give them hope. Can you communicate life to them? Hope and unity are woven together. I think unity is actually a spiritual thing, and it must be developed. As we remember contextually that missions is not a program, but the very heartbeat of God, we are likewise pressed to weave together the unique gifts to bring about meaningful opportunities for impact. Unity, as it breeds hope, is created when people care about their team's goal. Unity is created when people care about their teammates. The work of a team of church-going friends sharing faith with one another or with newfound friends, built through relationships and events, comes into focus when in their unity of friendship and purpose, hope is communicated to all. Unity is created when people care about their God and His purposes. Unity is created when people care about people.

> *"Unity is created when people care about their team and care about their teammates."*

### Key #4 (Lesson 30) Don't worry about the critics. You'll always have them.

*"Do not complain, brethren, against one another,*

*so that you yourselves may not be judged; behold, the Judge is standing right at the door." James 5:9 (NASB)*

Some simple and practical reminders on this matter will follow. If you're dealing with criticism, then don't let the wall keep you from seeing the road. Focus on the path ahead. Another way I heard it put recently, "Ignore the boos. They usually come from the cheap seats." Now, that may be a culturally contextualized analogy better understood in the rude environs of North American sports arenas, but the key is simply to recognize those criticizing you are rarely the ones called to understand the depth of the weights or responsibilities upon your shoulders.

Make the choices that are right. People will criticize you either way. Recognize, in the middle of your missional journey, your focus is still that of reaching the lost. There will be those who don't like what you do or how you do it. There will be those who will challenge you in doing it. Follow Him anyway.

> *"Make the choices that are right. People will criticize you either way."*

Follow the Father anyway. Follow the Spirit anyway. Follow your Savior anyway. Because He is standing at the door and He will take care of it all.

*"Do not judge, and you will not be judged; and do not condemn, and you will not be condemned;*

131

*pardon, and you will be pardoned. 38 Give, and it will be given to you. They will pour into your lap a good measure—pressed down, shaken together, and running over. For by your standard of measure it will be measured to you in return."*
Luke 6:37–38 (NASB)

## Key #5 (Lesson 32) Windows of opportunity don't last long.

Jesus taught us the standards of no procrastination—no backward look—you can't put God's Kingdom off until tomorrow—seize the day. Windows of opportunity will not last long. God is calling many in this house—this listening—this reading today to do a mighty work for Him. And when He speaks to your spirit about a specific thing—maybe a daily thing to share faith in the grocery or to take the

> *"Windows of opportunity will not last long."*

last money and give to missions or to give your best pair of shoes to the neighbor next door or to buy a t-shirt for a friend—it could be a simple daily thing like that or it could be something that may feel odd to you, like for you to go pray for this person and pray this prayer. "That doesn't make sense, Lord," you say. "They'll make fun of me, Lord. It's not the right environment, Lord." But, some know well *life is like a fleeting vapor* and then life changes. If He tells you to pray for me, pray for me now. Don't wait until tomorrow—seize the day. Because you don't know what will happen in my life or what I'm walking through. Tomorrow may be too late. Are you listening to Him? He's speaking.

Windows don't last long. When He calls upon me, if I don't walk through that door, He'll call someone else. Because *His ways are higher than mine, and His thoughts are deeper than mine.* He has a plan, and in perfect unity He's pulling the Body together and *His eyes,* as we've already said, *are going to and fro looking for a heart turned toward Him* so He can change the world. And He's going to use you to do it.

Just maybe it's a bigger thing like, "Go back to school and get ready." "Get ready for what, Lord? I still don't see it, Lord." "*My ways are higher than yours and my thoughts are deeper than yours.* Go back to school and get ready." And when He sees you walk in that faith, it's a part of the window to the world and then He will open the next step, which will change you, your children, and everyone you meet in the process.

If we don't walk through the doors of open opportunities because we're fearful or because we're prideful, we'll miss the cultural contextualization of what He's doing in your life. Remember, culture matters for you also. And contextualization matters for you, as well. Be in the center of His will.

So, when President Joseph Dimitrov received a degree in

law, in intellectual property, it didn't seem to make sense as of today because that's not what he's doing today. But he shared with me that when God called him into the ministry

> *"Your steps are ordered of God. Do not second-guess yourself."*

it was those very degrees that opened the doors for him. You are ordered of the Lord. Your steps are ordered of God. Do not second-guess yourself. God is in control of my life, my future, my family, and my children. His steps are upon me so that the feet of good news are blessed. Remember that for yourselves.

> *"So then, while we have opportunity, let us do good to all people, and especially to those who are of the household of the faith."* Galatians 6:10 (NASB)

> *"We must work the works of Him who sent Me as long as it is day; night is coming when no one can work."* John 9:4 (NASB)

> *"Jesus said, 'No procrastination. No backward looks. You can't put God's kingdom off till tomorrow. Seize the day.'"* Luke 9:62 (MSG)

**Key #6 (Lesson 44) Do not be in a hurry to leave the king's presence. Ecclesiastes 8:3 (NIV). It is the secret place.**

One of the best kept secrets of our faith is the devotion of ourselves to that "secret place" relationship with God. Like others, I too know what it's like to live "below" what the Christian life could be and should be. And, I know what it is like to feel almost powerless to change anything. But, comes…the secret place…and it changes all that. It changes everything!

Remember, just one touch, she thought to herself. If I could just touch His garment, I will be healed (Matt. 9). It's the secret place. It's in the secret place that we hear far more clearly and distinctly what God is saying to us through His Word and through His still small voice that still speaks to us today. It's in this secret place relationship that we learn the keys to change the person's life standing in front of us. Or, we learn the tools to change our very attitudes when He needs to put us back in line. It's in these secret place encounters with God that we interpret current events through the lens of God's Word. And, in this place we also quiet our hearts long enough to listen so that we are renewed by His deep love and callings for our lives.

> *"It's in the secret place that we hear far more clearly and distinctly what God is saying to us through His Word and through His still small voice that still speaks to us today."*

> *"You will show me the path of life; In Your presence is fullness of joy; At Your right hand are pleasures forevermore."* Psalm 16:11 (NKJV)

135

**Key #7 (Lesson 48) Everybody has a story.**

I've heard stories this morning. I've spoken with many of you in hallways, and I feel like you're friends. I've heard parts and pieces of your stories. I've shared small pieces of mine. Everybody has a story.

The Lord has spoken to me about some of your lives and it's helped me to understand you better. Everyone has gone through something that has changed them and we're promised in the Scripture...

> *"And we know that for those who love God all things work together for good, for those who are called according to his purpose."* Romans 8:28 (ESV)

Remind yourself of this. All the forces of darkness cannot stop what God has ordained. If God has ordained it, the enemy cannot change it. Because *He is high and lifted up and His train still fills the temple.* There is no other name under heaven but Jesus. He is the great I am, the provider and creator, redeemer of all things and all mankind. Every person has a story. And every person with a story is a life that can change the world. So don't judge people before you truly know them. The truth might surprise you. Everyone has gone through something that has changed their life— changed them—and completely turned their life from one direction to another. So, strive to listen to the stories.

Make an effort in conversations, hallway dialogues, phone calls, and family visits to answer briefly when people ask the familiar, "How are you doing?" Then, respond with something that will open up their world to you just a little bit more. Like, "I'd love to know more about your story. Tell me about it." Or, when people aren't expecting it, make the effort to pause the direction of your conversations and quite simply inquire about their children, or their grandchildren, or what might be new in their lives. Show people you care about them and about theirs. That is the most rich and rewarding thing we can do to care about people. It leads us to relationship, which leads us to...missional pneumatology through cultural contextualization.

> *"And every person with a story is a life that can change the world. So don't judge people before you truly know them. The truth might surprise you."*

Now, let's look at the others, but very briefly. As an American, some of my analogies are culturally, contextually relevant for me as an American. In whatever country or culture you are from, you can consider analogies more fitting for your contexts. Those listening or reading this piece are likely intellectually prone and to some extent theological students. These are my fifty. I challenge you to create your own fifty. That's not a joke. Because the story that you share—from Italy, to Pakistan, to Cameroon, to France, to Belgium, or wherever—will be riddled with your own cultural illustrations, as is mine, but it will be contextually relevant for that moment for those people you encounter so that you might just find yourself positioned by God to change the world. So, I share with you some of mine...

## 50 Missional Lessons Learned in 30+ Years of Ministry

*"My goal is that they may be encouraged in heart and united in love, so that they may have the full riches of complete understanding, in order that they may know the mystery of God, namely, Christ, 3 in whom are hidden all the treasures of wisdom and knowledge."* Colossians 2:2–3 (NIV)

### #1 We all need a purpose.
Everyone needs to find a purpose. What is your goal? What is your ministry about? When it's said and done, if I have an epitaph on a tombstone, it only needs to say, "He loved. He loved his wife. He loved his children. And, he loved his God, who changed his life." Have a purpose.

### #2 May life never steal your dreaming.
Cultural contextualization: These things matter when sharing the gospel. Never let life steal your dreams. Be able

to dream. Be able to dream for yourself so you can dream for others. Life wants to steal dreaming; don't let it happen. Get a dream and go after it. Without vision the people perish, the Bible says. Be light in darkness. Don't dwell on the past. The Prophet Isaiah taught us to "forget the former things" (43:18, NIV). We should pray to God that He help us not measure services by how many people attend, or by how many are at an altar, or by whatever measure of mere numbers, but by how many lives are actually being changed. John Wesley was asked, it's said, as to why so many people came to hear him preach. His answer was, "...because I set myself on fire and they come to watch me burn." Dream God-sized dreams, friends. And, burn hot for Christ.

> *"Never let life steal your dreams."*

### #3 You are called to heal the broken-hearted.
You must know a broken heart to know how to minister to the broken-hearted (Isa. 61). I need to know a broken heart before I can heal it. As an example, sometimes you have to get outside your box, knock on doors, or walk down streets and place flyers. You will not know what you will learn about those houses you've walked by unless you have first accepted the task of simply walking the street to place flyers. Then God takes the next step and puts you in the very place He's looking for a Spirit-filled woman or man

> *"You must know a broken heart to know how to minister to the broken-hearted."*

of God. But, it starts with serving someone. You're healed and you're called to heal the broken-hearted, and you need to know some broken hearts before you can heal them.

## #4 You can learn from anyone.

The key is to want to. Put it in your spirit that whoever is in front of you—no matter how bad that professor is (laughter)—you can learn from anyone. You can learn from... anyone. No matter how wealthy they are, you belong in their world. You are a child of the King. Hold your head high and wear the aroma of the Lord. No matter how poor they may be, you can learn from any-one, because we are all children of the King. Remember, do more listening—and observing—than posturing. You can learn from anyone. The key is to want to.

> *"You can learn from anyone. The key is to want to."*

## #5 The essential element for church growth is vision.

A church will start to die when it decides to keep people instead of reach people. So the key to church growth is vision. May we always reach people and never find ourselves worried about keeping people. I have also found through the years that cream rises to the top. And in that context, everything is relative. When your best workers, your best team members, your strongest leaders—those you need the most—are called somewhere else, the missionary call, then release them. Again, remember God's ways are higher than ours and deeper than ours. If He has called for one, then you can be totally convinced He has already spoken to another to come along your side to meet the need. And, in unity, we will all work together in His callings to win the world for Christ.

> *"When your best workers, your best team members, your strongest leaders—those you need the most—are called somewhere else, the missionary call, then release them."*

## # 6 There is no substitute for leadership.

If you don't lead by example, you don't lead. These are American contextualizations.

a. American soldier General George Patton: *"Accept the challenges so you may feel the exhilaration of victory."*

b. Baseball player Babe Ruth: *"It's hard to beat a person who never gives up."*

c. President Harry Truman: *"To be able to lead others, [one] must be willing to go forward alone."*

    i. Sometimes you're the only one in your family walking forward. You're the only one bowing your heart to Jesus, the only one hearing the pounding of your heart to reach the nations. Follow it. To whom much is given, much is required. There are few

true leaders in life, and the ones filled with the
spirit of God will change the world.

d.  Conqueror, defeated at Waterloo (Belgium), Napoleon
Bonaparte is famous for saying, "The word impossible
is not in my dictionary."

e.  President Theodore Roosevelt: "I dream of men who
take the next step rather than worrying about the
thousand steps beyond."

i.  One step at a time. Every step is a step of faith. And
every step takes you closer to His glory.

## #7 May tears flow again, for souls.

May fathers, may pastors, never see the day when tears do
not flow from their own hearts for a lost and dying world.
Never be afraid of your emotion. Or of the spirit of God

> *"Never be afraid of your emotion."*

upon your life, or the moment when He
catches you off guard. Though some
won't say it or want to admit it, there
are times eyes tear up as hearts are
burdened. May you never lose that—
ever. When you're away from your family doing what He's
called of you, don't lose that. Have you ever taken enough
time to be in the secret place long enough that you actually
cry over your family that you've left—or that you are not
with—that they might hear what you hear, see what you see,
and feel what you feel? Sure, you cry because you miss
them, but that's not what I'm addressing. Do you cry that
they might know what God is revealing to you?

**#8 We need a fresh revelation**.

I've spoken briefly a part of my testimony. My mother left when I was small child, and other than a few times in my life I never saw her again until she died. But I didn't tell you the rest of the story. My God is a Redeemer. So—I lived with my father. He couldn't cook. And he couldn't be a mother, though he tried. I remember crying many nights, a little boy missing his mother. And then some years later my father met this wonderful Christian woman. She had likewise been divorced, not of her own choosing, and now lived humbly and as if she were married to Jesus. She read the Word, prayed, and was faithfully involved in her church. She was a very simple woman with only an eighth-grade education, with eleven siblings (I think), who had had to drop out of school to help support her family. But she loved her God. One day she came home and became my mother. For the rest of my life, my stepmother became my mom. I have a great respect for stepmoms. It's one thing to birth a child, another thing to be a father. Or, another thing to be a mother. She loved me as her own. She died of cancer a few years ago, and I called her Mom. At my mom's deathbed, I was at her side. Both my mothers—she, my stepmom, as well as that of my maternal mother—at their deathbeds. But this one was really my mom, and just hours the day before she died, she looks at me and says, "It's time." "It's time for what, Mom?" "It's time to die." "Are you worried... fearful? scared?" "No, I just wanted you to know." She'd had a revelation. She just wanted me to know. And when you've had a revelation to change the world, they need to know. When you've had a revelation from God, you need to tell somebody. You need to walk up to them and tell somebody. You need not be fearful. I just want you to know. Change the world, Church. Change the world, Church. Did I say, "Change the world, Church"? It's all about cultural contextualization. When you're

> *"When you've had a revelation, the world needs to know it."*

standing in front of someone's life, don't frivolously or uncaringly try to tell them something. When you've had a revelation, the world needs to know it.

## # 9 Pastors must allow people to be people; don't expect saints.

We are all under construction, even the pastors. So, if you're studying to be pastors (and some of you are ladies) by faith you, too, can be pastors. (In my state of Kentucky, one-fourth of the ministerial credential holders in the denomination I

> *"And, when the people don't live up to your standards, love them anyway."*

serve are women. So don't sell yourself too short, ladies; God has a plan. Some of you ladies may be pastors' wives; some of you may be children's or youth pastors, or lead pastors or church planters. For those men who are challenged with the fact that a woman could minister God's truth, just remember this fact. It was the faithfulness of women preachers that gave the world the knowledge of the

Resurrection. Now, that's something to think about, isn't it?) But, the key is pastors must allow people to be people. Don't expect saints. Too often pastors expect their congregations to be spiritually enlightened so they will follow the Word of God. But sheep need a shepherd. That's why God is calling us to be shepherds. So teach the Word—the whole Word—and be not ashamed of it. You didn't write it, you just preach it. And let Him do His work. And, when the people don't live up to your standards, love them anyway. Every mother and father loves their children, but they don't disregard them when they choose not to listen that day. You nurture them more, so

> "I spent a secluded three days at the Abbey of Gethsemani, a Trappist monastery in Kentucky."

they learn to hear their mother's and father's voices. Pastors need to let people be people. Because we're all under construction and sheep need a shepherd.

## # 10 "Be still, and know that I am God." Psalm 46:10 (KJV). Learn solitude.

It will lower your blood pressure and bring peace to your life. We don't understand solitude much these days. But it is cultural contextualization. For me to know what God is speaking for that moment, for that nation, for that mission, for this opportunity, for this person, I need to be in His presence and I need to hear His presence. Hear His presence? Yes. I must hear His voice. Be still and know that I am God. Find time for spiritual solitude. When I began my doctoral studies, a required assignment in an initial class was to find a place of solitude. I spent a secluded three days at the Abbey of Gethsemani, a Trappist monastery in Kentucky. It was there that famed French-born friar Thomas Merton lived and served. There, the monks live in silence, with the exception of their various services and liturgical songs and prayers. They are on a journey of joyfully understanding and living the mystery of Christ-

> "We would all be well-served in this world of instant everything to journey a little closer toward the contemplative."

among-us. We would all be well-served in this world of instant everything to journey a little closer toward the contemplative.

## #11 The battle is not yours, but the Lord's (2 Chronicles 20:15)

Satan has no weapon that can penetrate the breastplate of righteousness. The devil will always try to diminish you in an attempt to minimize your influence. No matter what the weapon, you win. The battle is not yours, it's the Lord's. Raising funds is not your problem. It's the Lord's. My future—not my problem. My family scenario—not my problem. It's the Lord's. Now, don't misunderstand. Work with me here. We all have responsibilities. But, I gave my life to Him. (For me, at an altar in 1982. My life was a mess. And I went to the right side of the altar. I had sat in the very back of the church, in the last seat of the row, right inside a side door. And it was there—for the first time—I sensed the tangible presence of God. I had grown up in a home with a mother and father who loved me and who taught me about God, but at that moment my life was a mess. "Lord, I need you," I said. "My life is a mess. Come to me and turn it around." The problems were not mine. They were His. And from that moment forward, I got up from that place knowing when I got up my culture was still the same, my friends were still the same, my work was still the same, my apartment where I lived was still the same, but I knew I was no longer driving. I had a Savior in control of my life. Day-by-day, step-by-step, moment-by-moment, faith-by-faith, He took control of my life's journey. And, I allowed Him to direct me. I soon then met the most beautiful gazelle I had ever met in my life. And she changed my life. [Laughter.])

> *"Day-by-day, step-by-step, moment-by-moment, faith-by-faith, He took control of my life's journey."*

### # 12 *"[Love] beareth all things, [Love] believeth all things, [Love] endureth all things, [Love] hopeth all things."* **1 Corinthians 13:7 (KJV)**

Cultural contextualization: When you look at people...love bears, believes, and hopes all things. No matter who they are, what they believe or don't believe. Love people. And let God be God. He didn't call you to save them. He called you to love them. He didn't call you to save them. He called you to serve them. He didn't call you to save them. He called you to give them truth. Let Him do His work. But *the harvest is plenteous and the laborers are few*. Who will say, "Here am I, send me. Send me. I will go"? Simply, love.

## # 13 God has not called me to be successful. He's called me to be faithful.

Corrie ten Boom said,

> *"Never be afraid to trust an unknown future to a known God."*

There are many who will try to define success to you. There will always be those who will have a sense of whether or not you are being and doing as they deem successful. But, remember, you didn't accept the call to answer to people's inclinations of what they

> *"He didn't call you to save them. He called you to serve them."*

want from you. The called answer, ultimately, those life questions to God himself. You can't always fix things, and fixing them doesn't define whether or not you're actually successful, though it's easy to get caught up in that kind of thinking. A friend of mine from Kentucky, Clayton Arp, a national ministry director, said something to me once that I've never forgotten and I've often quoted it to myself and others. It's a great reminder to me at times when I'm struggling to

> *"I didn't cause it. I can't control it. And I can't cure it. But, I know Who can."*

determine if I'm making a difference.

> *"I didn't cause it. I can't control it. And I can't cure it. But, I know Who can."* Clayton Arp

It helps remind me that I am not called to define success as others would so define it. I'm simply—and beautifully—called to faithfulness. God will do the rest.

**# 14 Perception is reality to the people who have it.**
Maturity means discerning truth and avoiding error. Cultural contextualization: You cannot change people's perceptions. Whatever perception they have, they have. Don't worry about the critics; they'll always be there. Do the right thing anyway. Perception is reality—to the people who have it. For the people who looked at Helen Keller—the blind and deaf woman walking down the hall—those unwilling to recognize she was the most educated woman in America at the time, unwilling to recognize she had more truth in her heart than anyone else in the room. For those who look at Americans and judge them all the same, perception is reality to the people who have it. To those who look at Africans and have a perception, it is reality to the people who have it. Or to those who look at Muslims and have a perception, perception is reality to the people

> *"Too often Christians, I think, put expectations upon people who are not believers that are ridiculous and unfounded."*

who have it. You can't change perception. God didn't call me to change your perception. He called me to follow Him. Your perception is your issue. But, my response to your perception is most definitely my issue. It's one that I must learn to process with godly character. Your perception is as it is, but I will choose to love you, regardless. I have no problem loving the unbeliever. I have no problem choosing to not get bent out of shape when non-Christians act or speak, or respond or react, as they actually should—like non-Christians. Too often Christians, I think, put expectations upon people who are not believers that are ridiculous and unfounded, for the simple reason that they are worldly. When you think about it, it's totally natural for non-Christians to be, speak, act, and respond, in manners that are worldly. So, recognize it and accept it. People have perceptions. And, perception is reality to the people who have it.

## # 15 Let integrity set your standards, and never apologize for standards.

Now, compared to #14, this is where often the rubber meets the road, as we say in the USA. Accepting people for who they are is one thing. But, there is an important journey to finding that fine line where you must—with integrity and with standards and with principles—stand up for Christ. If a "Christ-ian" doesn't, who will? In the process of it all, do what you do with integrity. Your integrity will speak to those you minister to. They are reading, perceiving, and learning from you.

In the USA we have the holiday of Thanks-giving. Renee, this past Thanks-giving, had ordered two turkeys for our meal which had about twenty-three people joining us in our home. They were living with us for the entire week. I didn't have to cook the turkeys, but my job was to go get them. So, I went to the grocery that morning, picked up the turkeys as instructed, went to the checkout counter, and paid the bill. Upon returning home and delivering the items, Renee noticed the receipt had only billed us for one of the turkeys, not both. Calling it to my attention, she immediately instructed me to return to the grocery—about five to six miles across town. So, I did.

> *"Let your integrity set your standards."*

Explaining it to the manager at the counter, he double-checked the bill. I said that when I had checked out, I had double asked the person at the register if that was all of the total and they assured me it was, but...then he smiled and said, "Your wife was correct, the person at the checkout counter had only charged you for one. But, I am surely not accustomed to customers returning and being so honest. Because of your honesty, I am only going to charge you half price for the second turkey. Thank you for being honest. And, enjoy your Thanksgiving." I believe that my wife's integrity spoke more to that man that day than it did to any of us in our home. Let your integrity set your standards.

**# 16 When in doubt, don't.** Some people say, "Yes." Others say, "Do." Or others say, "Go." But, as one who has

151

been in the secret place, you will hear His voice. When in doubt, don't. There is a perfect timing for everything. And if it is His will He will show you when it is right. Hear from God and say, "Thus saith the Lord." But, only say it when you're certain He's directed it. (I've always been leery of those super-Christians who are constantly saying, "God told me…" this or that. So, don't say that, if you're not certain it's from Him. When in doubt, don't.) Further, many struggle determining God's perfect will for their lives, or how to respond to a specific situation, or whether or not they should do "this or that." Renee and I have always been goal-oriented. In our early years together, we set short-term and life goals, hoping to help us stay focused as life got busy. For decades in our marriage, we've always agreed when it comes to any decision for our lives, our family, or our marriage: "When in doubt, don't."

## # 17 Do more listening and observing than posturing.

This was looked at in some detail earlier. But the next point reminds us…

## # 18 God has divine amnesia.

May we always remember He throws your sins away as far as the east is from the west, never to be remembered again. And what the devil keeps bringing to your heart and mind (those sins of your past many times repented of and taken to the Lord in sorrow),

*"God has divine amnesia."*

152

your Jesus doesn't see it anymore. He doesn't know it exists. He threw it away so the devil could never use it against you in the eternal glories. And, someday, He will say, *"Enter in...well done...good and faithful servant."* He will go to the Father and say "He/she is mine." God has divine amnesia. Don't give the devil more credit that he is due.

## # 19 If my wife still loves me and my kids are okay, I'm okay.

It is quite possible that I—to this day—give this answer in response to someone at least four or five times a week when asked the standard and casual, "How are you doing?"

> *"If my wife still loves me and my kids are okay, I'm okay."*

question. I can give my life to serve Him, but my life is no good without reliability. And, the most precious gift He gives you is your family. Stay true. Israel committed spiritual adultery. Stay true. Stay true. Stay true to your children. Stay true to your spouse. And, if they still love you, you're okay.

## # 20 If your walk with God isn't the priority, nothing else matters.

First Corinthians 1:18–19 says,

> *"For the message of the cross is foolishness to those who are perishing, but to us who are being saved it is the power of God. ¹⁹ For it is written: I will destroy the wisdom of the wise; the intelligence of*

153

*the intelligent I will frustrate." 1* Corinthians 1:18–19 (NIV)

For those who do not know a personal relationship with Christ, every excuse in the world has been used for why they choose to not follow Him. The bottom line is found in Acts 4:12,

> ""Salvation is found in no one else, for there is no other name under heaven given to mankind by which we must be saved."

> *"Salvation is found in no one else, for there is no other name under heaven given to mankind by which we must be saved." Acts 4:12 (NIV)*

## # 21 If I don't take care of my walk with God, no one else will.

That's why one's faith walk is personal. The only one who can commit to search, genuinely and fully read God's Word to learn and comprehend what's in it, pray and talk to the Creator of the universe and all life, study the major doctrines of Christianity, determine the faith understanding and worship community God desires for me, repent and accept God—or deny and walk away from God—is me.

## # 22 Sometimes it is necessary to say, "No." If I don't guard my time, no one else will and wasted time is irretrievable. We live in a culture of "yes." Only when one

learns to say "no" can they take control of their own lives, calendars, schedules, and priorities, in light of God's direction for their lives. And, trust me, seemingly everyone will want to direct for you how to use the hours in your day, your week, or your month. As the years go by, the calendars will often control you. Don't let that occur if you're living in those years of "go, go, go." Sometimes, you're allowed to say, "no."

> "Sometimes, you're allowed to say, 'no.'"

## # 23 Disappointment is part of the price tag for leadership.

It's okay. Disappointment will not kill you; just expect it. Many people will not live up to your expectations. Love them anyway. Cultural contextualization: The person you're in front of—love them anyway. Love them anyway. Love them anyway. Family members, church members, colleagues, peers, pastors, leaders, teachers, professors, physicians, or attorneys, remember—people disappoint. Only God delights, encourages, and satisfies with certainty and truth.

## # 24 Work off priorities.

Determine what's important for your day. Write it down if you need to. Keep it in a calendar if you need to. Why? Because windows of opportunity don't last long. If He's told you to do something, put it on your calendar. Put it on your timeframe. As an example, you might write down, "Within this week, I will accomplish this, or within this month—or within this year—or within this season..." But, in the big picture, I see where I'm going. I will not make steps today that steal my dreams. If He redirects them, I am a servant in His care. But for now, I have dreams He's put in my heart, and I will not make decisions now that keep me from accomplishing them. For now, I will work off priorities.

**# 25 There is no substitute for good communication**. Already talked about in great detail.

**# 26 Put your family before your work.** In some years recent, a previous general superintendent of the Assemblies of God USA, a formidable man in every way, Rev. Thomas Trask, had welcomed me to a meeting in his private office. It was a very important meeting. In the USA you don't get invited to the general superintendent's office very often. But that day, there I stood. My cell phone rang. Respectfully, it was on vibrate. But, I pulled it out to look and see it was my teenage son. I

> *"Put your family before your work."*

loved him more than my life itself, and I think he knew that. I had always taught our kids they would forever be able to get me, so I kindly apologized to the superintendent, and said, "I need to take this."

I answered the phone, stepping into the hallway. It was something insignificant that he was wanting or asking, likely only wanting something for baseball practice...but it was important to him. And, to me, it was the most significant and pertinent call and moment of my day. I said, "Excuse me, sir. And I won't take any other calls, but I have promised to always take the calls of my wife and my children." So, I answered that call. My son knew I was always his—and regardless of who's presence I was in, I was so proud of him and would always make myself available for his well-being. I've always done the same for my daughter. Our kids are only little once. Pour everything you've got into them. If you lose your family, none of this matters, none of this counts. Put your family before your work. If you do not, in all practicality, you will lose your true ministry anyway.

> *"Our kids are only little once. Pour everything you've got into them."*

## # 27 Not everyone has pure motives.

The people God calls you to may or may not have pure motives. Having spent a career and lifetime in the ministry, I can honestly say it is one of the most difficult things to come to grips with, meeting with people, other Christians or even those who serve as pastors or church leaders, and finding out their intentions are less than faithful. He didn't call you to change their motives. He called you to love them, counsel or direct them, and serve them—so He might change them.

## # 28 Expect God to do exceedingly abundantly more than you can ask or think.

Nothing is impossible with God—Luke 1:37 (NLT). His

faithfulness is beyond anything human reasoning can comprehend. When you learn to trust in Him, you will begin to see His daily working in your life for your good and for His glory.

## # 29 Unity has to be developed and then guarded at all costs.

This was also looked at in some detail earlier. The enemy loves nothing more than to bring division into your life, your family, your relationships, and your faith in God. Ephesians 4:3 tells us to:

> *"Make every effort to keep the unity of the Spirit through the bond of peace"*
> *Ephesians 4:3 (NIV)*

> *"Make every effort to keep the unity of the Spirit through the bond of peace."* Ephesians 4:3 (NIV)

## # 30 Don't worry about the critics. You'll always have them.

Again, this too was looked at in some detail earlier.

## # 31 There's no substitute for loyalty.

It seems to me few are loyal today to systems, organizations, churches, governments, methods, denominations, or even their lifelong sports teams. Loyalty is a changing allegiance. But, to me, and maybe it's demo-graphically defined for each of us, there is little more significant and vital than loyalty. If you find a loyal friend, a loyal team member, or a loyal employee, you've found a treasure. Protect it. Protect them.

## # 32 Windows of opportunity don't last long.
And, again... This was looked at in detail previously.

## # 33 If you do something wrong, admit it, apologize for it, and move on.
Too many in today's world are too proud to admit their mistakes. Too many refuse to humble themselves just enough to be real and build bridges when they've spent months or years tearing them down. When you've messed up, admit it. God forgives. People will, too. Especially, dads and moms should be more transparent with their children, and each of us should be likewise to and with our families. It takes your interactions to another level when your transparency is genuine and given in true humility. The precious look in the eyes of a child seeing their parents admit they are not perfect gives them the freedom to grow and develop in the light of the beauty of Christ's love and in the midst of all of our own weaknesses. Man up. Humble yourselves. Apologize. Repent. Move on.

> *"The precious look in the eyes of a child seeing their parents admit they are not perfect gives them the freedom to grow and develop in the light of the beauty of Christ's love and in the midst of all of our own weaknesses."*

# # 34 God gives second chances, and so should we.

Related to #33, if people will forgive (and they will,) remember, so will God. When someone hurts you, disappoints you, or fails you, take it the Lord and never cut them off. It's not worth losing the opportunity to someday, somehow impact them for Christ. Build the bridges, and give them another chance. How many times? Seventy times seven. In Matthew, Jesus says that church associates should pardon each other "seventy times seven times" (18:22), a quantity that denotes boundlessness.

# # 35 Joy is not dependent upon circumstances.

I can choose how I will respond. I can choose to trust in God's Word and His promises. I can choose love and faith. I can't control others or often what occurs to me or mine, but I can choose to trust God—always.

> *"My flesh and my heart may fail, but God is the strength of my heart and my portion forever."*
> Psalm 73:26, (NIV)

# # 36 No matter how I perceive the circumstances around me, God is still in control.

Some of Satan's most prevalent weaponries are fear and anxiety. *God is our refuge and strength*, we're told in Psalm 46:1, *an ever-present help in trouble* (NIV).

# # 37 There's no substitute for hard work.

If you want to attain your dreams, you must write those

essays; there is no substitute for hard work. When others show up at 9 a.m., you show up at 7. When others pray for thirty minutes, you pray for an hour. When others carry ten bricks, you carry twenty.

## # 38 A nation's government does not understand the ways of God.

On March 6, 1857, the most dismaying decision from the US Supreme Court ruled in the Dred Scott case that "negroes were less than human." On January 22, 1973, the Supreme Court decided *Roe vs. Wade*, and I've heard it said that now 60 to 70 million pre-born babies have been killed. Christians must pray, vote, and be the voice for those who cannot speak for themselves. Be the voice for those who cannot speak.

> *"Be the voice for those who cannot speak."*

## # 39 Regarding the US Supreme Court Decision *Roe vs. Wade*, abortion is not the problem. Sexual sin is the problem.

(1 Cor. 6:9–10, 6:13, 6:18; Gal. 5:19; 1 Thess. 4:3).

## # 40 Where sin abounds, grace much more abounds (Rom 5:20).

God's grace is truly amazing. So many have forgotten that simple promise. I've always felt that people who have been forgiven for much understand grace at a much deeper level. And, those who have had little need—in their journey or in their understanding—of grace have the hardest time accepting it. To whom much is forgiven, grace is truly amazing.

> *"To whom much is forgiven, grace is truly amazing."*

## # 41 We don't need another revival service.

We need an Azusa-like "visitation." When I was a child, I remember churches would often have weeklong revival services. When I entered the pastorate, those multiple weeklong revivals were fewer and less accepted. Today, those types of revival services are nearly unheard of. Gratefully, in Kentucky and across the Americas, there is a surge in spiritual hunger and a number of locations where revivals such as these are making a comeback. It is important to remember the services themselves are not revival. It's the changing of lives and communities that defines revival. The supernatural, the manifest presence of God, and signs and wonders still follow those who believe.

## # 42 Spurgeon said, *"God will not use a man that He has first not undone."*

Earlier in this book, I spoke to some degree regarding brokenness. It's more important than I could ever express. Only in my humility and brokenness can I see the glory and wholeness of life in Christ.

## # 43 God's mountains are worth climbing.

Moses climbed Sinai and saw God (Exod. 19). He climbed

Mt. Nebo and saw the Promised Land (Deut. 34:1–6). I know we'll face mountains in our lives. There certainly have been some in mine. Climb them. God will meet you there.

## # 44 *"Do not be in a hurry to leave the king's presence."* Ecclesiastes 8:3 (NIV) It's the secret place.

This, as one of the initial seven items we addressed, was looked at in some detail earlier.

## # 45 Serve others.

God will never forget it.

> *"God is not unjust; he will not forget your work and the love you have shown Him as you have helped His people and continue to help them."* Hebrews 6:10 (NIV).

My wife has an undeniable and remarkable gift of hospitality. I wish every church and every Christian could be the same. It certainly would enhance the church's chances of keeping those guests. And, if I were the neighbor to a friend like this, I'd likely not feel too awkward about returning for another evening of laughter and friendship. It is relationships with friends that lead the searching or open heart to the things of God. In addressing serving others, I want to add this simple but profound truth to the mix of the conversation. The greatest thing anyone can do for another is lift his or her name to God in prayer. I've learned the art of prayer from my wife, Renee. She is a faithful woman of prayer. Through the years of our marriage, it became custom for "Mom" to lead our family in prayers at the dinner table. Now, before you judge me for being a poor example of the "man of the home," you have to remember every family has "context" to the rhythms and rhymes of what and why for their lives.

Renee keeps things in balance for me. She loves to pray, and I love hearing her pray. She is serving her family and honoring us the most as she prays for us. So, pray for others. It's a rich way of serving them. And, when praying for global workers, missionaries around the world, include in your prayers wisdom, favor, anointing, health, protection, financial supply, protection in spiritual warfare, and prayers for their children. While it's likely the minimum, a great start, and far more can still be done in the physical, there is no better way to serve than prayer.

> *"While it's likely the minimum, a great start, and far more can still be done in the physical, there is no better way to serve than prayer."*

## # 46 You can only talk convincingly about the God you know.

> *"His face glowed from being in the presence of the God."* Exodus 34:29 (TLB).

If you've ever been to a wedding where the bride and groom

simply adored one-another, you've seen the look in their eyes as the groom watches the beautifully adorned bride walk down the aisle. It's a glow that no one could miss. Have you ever been to the airport and waited for your friend to arrive? I have stood there many times and watched perfect strangers run and embrace with "that glow" of love saying, "I've missed you so."

I've heard people recite studied passages or speeches. I've even heard people stand to pray in public worship services and begin to deliver well-memorized prayers. I've seen and heard singers and musicians, who would be better served with the title of performers from my perspective. Someone who knows from personal relationship the God they worship will always get my attention. They offer a "glow" that's unmistakable. I think it's the simple, non-assuming anointing found only in intimacy of the secret place. When you know God that way, people will take notice and listen.

> *"They offer a "glow" that's unmistakable. I think it's the simple, non-assuming anointing found only in intimacy of the secret place."*

### # 47 Make others more important than yourself — always.

I remember, as a child, when it started to occur to me that our family might be less affluent than others. There were school children that it dawned on me were treating me differently, as if I were poor. I remember the feeling when the big yellow school bus would drop off other children in front of large brick homes and asphalted driveways and then stop in front of our home, modest as it was, for all to watch me walk up the long gravel driveway. Then, as an adult, I remember being in the presence of individuals that quite simply carried an air, a manner, a tone about them that consciously or sometimes subconsciously, looked down at others or myself because they or I weren't from their "class."

Or, the times when speaking with another leader, they were so busy with what they were doing they opted to not even take the time to stand to greet someone, to shake their hand, or to look them in the eye. It appalled me and to this day is one of the criteria classifying to me those who will not become confidants or friends. Always make others more important than yourselves. Always.

> *"Always make others more important than yourselves. Always."*

## # 48 To win the hearts of man, you must ask, and care, about his children.

I've always loved children. From the time they were newborns until they entered school, I enjoyed to the fullest a day off each week that was "dad's day." It was their day to pick anything they wanted to wear, what they wanted to eat (within reason), and what they wanted to do with dad that day. Those are wonderful memories.

Language, race, nationality, and religion aside, I've found

through the years most people across the world are all the same. We love our kids. If some-one wants to gain my respect, they'll care—genuinely care—about what's important to me. Care about their kids. To win the hearts of man, you must ask and genuinely care, about his children.

> *"To win the hearts of man, you must ask and genuinely care, about his children."*

## # 49 There is no substitute for a holy life.

> *"Daniel purposed in his heart that he would not defile himself"* Daniel 1:8 (KJV).

Taken by the armies of Nebuchadnezzar, this teenage Hebrew boy received a crash course in culture shock and cultural contextualization. His integrity of character and commitment to the God of his fathers led him to be the premier prophet during the era of captivity. In those moments when the enemy tempts and taunts, purpose that you will flee all appearance of evil so as not to defile yourself. You are being molded for royalty. Don't let the enemy steal that from you.

> *"You are being molded for royalty. Don't let the enemy steal that from you."*

Finally, also reviewed in detail before,
**# 50 Everybody has a story.**

Our society is under-challenged. Challenge people to change. So, as I close, I challenge you today. Do more listening than observing and posturing. Season your communication. Develop unity and protect it. Don't worry about your critics. They'll always be there. Walk through open doors. Windows of opportunity don't last long. Don't be in a hurry to leave God's presence. It's the secret place of anointing. Know your mission. *Everyone has a story. Find it.*

Jesus is calling, softly and tenderly Jesus is calling. "Calling for you and for me. See on the portals, He's waiting and watching; Watching for you and for me. Come home, come home; Ye who are weary come home. Earnestly, tenderly Jesus is calling; Calling, "O Sinner come home."

> *"Everyone has a story. Find it."*

Renee and I are honored to have been with you. Thank you.

> *"The Lord bless thee, and keep thee: 25 The Lord make his face shine upon thee, and be gracious unto thee: 26 The Lord lift up his countenance upon thee, and give thee peace."* Numbers 6:24–26 (KJV)

Truly, it is our heart to yours, "May the Lord richly put His hand upon your lives, and may you change the world."

# See Other Books by Joseph S. Girdler

*Setting the Atmosphere for the Day of Worship*.
Crestwood, KY: Meadow Stream Publishing, 2019
Girdler, Joseph S.

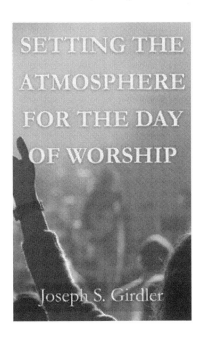

# Bibliography

Arn, Win, and Charles Arn. *The Master's Plan for Making Disciples: How Every Christian Can Be an Effective Witness through an Enabling Church*. Pasadena, CA: Church Growth Press, 1982.

Auch, Ron, and Dean Niforatos. *The Jesus Sensitive Church*. Green Forest, AR: New Leaf Press, 2006.

Barna, George. *Building Effective Lay Leadership Teams*. Ventura, CA: Issachar Resources, 2001.

Barna, George. *Growing True Disciples*. Colorado: Waterbrook Press, 2001.

Barton, Ruth Haley. *Invitation to Solitude and Silence: Experiencing God's Transforming Presence*. Downers Grove, IL: InterVarsity, 2010.

Blackaby, Henry, and Richard Blackaby. *Spiritual Leadership: Moving People on to God's Agenda*. Nashville: B&H, 2011.

Bonheoffer, Dietrich. *The Cost of Discipleship*. London

UK: SCM Press, 1959

Carpenter, Eugene, and Philip Comfort. *Holman Treasury of Key Bible Words: 200 Greek and 200 Hebrew Words Defined and Explained*. Nashville: Broadman and Holman, 2000. Logos Bible Software.

Clay, Doug. Assemblies of God USA General Superintendent, Kentucky Leadership Conference, Crestwood, KY, August 14, 2018.

Clowney, Edmund P. *Preaching and Biblical Theology*. Phillipsburg, NJ: P&R, 2002.

Cordeiro, Wayne. *Leading on Empty: Refilling Your Tank and Renewing Your Passion*. Minneapolis, MN: Bethany House, 2009.

Cymbala, Jim. *Spirit Rising*. Grand Rapids, MI: Zondervan, 2012.

Ferguson, Sinclair B. *By Grace Alone: How the Grace of God Amazes Me*. Orlando, FL: Reformation Trust Publishing, 2010.

Garrison, Alton. Assemblies of God USA Assistant General Superintendent, National AG Executives Conference, San Antonio, TX, November 6, 2018.

Girdler, Joseph S. *Setting the Atmosphere for the Day of Worship*. Crestwood, KY: Meadow Stream Publishing, 2019.

Grant, Beth. Assemblies of God USA, Executive Presbyter, National AG Executives Conference, San Antonio, TX, November 7, 2018.

Joiner, Reggie, Lane Jones, and Andy Stanley. *The 7 Practices of Effective Ministry*. Sisters, OR: Multnomah, 2004.

Lucado, Max. *A Gentle Thunder: Hearing God Through the Storm*. Nashville: Thomas Nelson, 2009.

Ravenhill, Leonard. *Why Revival Tarries*. Minnesota: Bethany House Publishers, 1959

Rhoden, Bob. *Four Faces of a Leader: What It Takes to Move Your Church Forward*. Springfield, MO: My Healthy Church, 2013.

Robeck, Cecil M., Jr. *The Azusa Street Mission and Revival: The Birth Of the Global Pentecostal Movement*. Nashville: Thomas Nelson, 2006.

Sinek, Simon. *Leaders Eat Last: Why Some Teams Pull Together and Others Don't*. New York: Penguin, 2014.

Sjogren, Steve. *The Perfectly Imperfect Church: Redefining the "Ideal" Church.* Loveland, CO: Group Publishing, 2002.

Sorge, Bob. *Secrets of the Secret Place: Keys to Igniting Your Personal Time with God.* Lee's Summit, MO: Oasis House, 2001.

Stamps, Donald. "Moral Qualifications of Overseers." In *NIV Life in the Spirit Study Bible.* Grand Rapids, MI: Zondervan, 2003.

-----"The Prophet in the Old Testament." In *NIV Life in the Spirit Study Bible.* Grand Rapids, MI: Zondervan, 2003.

-----"Study Notes on Revelation 1:1." In *NIV Life in the Spirit Study Bible.* Grand Rapids, MI: Zondervan, 2003.

Tennant, Carolyn. *Catch the Wind of the Spirit: How the 5 MINISTRY GIFTS can Transform Your Church.* Springfield: Vital Resources. 2016.

Stanley, Andy. *Visioneering: God's Blueprint for Developing and Maintaining Personal Vision.* Sisters, OR: Multnomah, 1999.

Surratt, Geoff. *Ten Stupid Things That Keep Churches*

*from Growing: How Leaders Can Overcome Costly Mistakes*. Grand Rapids, MI: Zondervan, 2009.

Swindoll, Charles R. *Improving Your Serve: The Art of Unselfish Living*. Nashville: Thomas Nelson, 1984.

Van Rheenan, G., and A. Parker. *Missions: biblical foundations and contemporary strategies*. 2nd ed. Grand Rapids, MI: Zondervan, 2014.

Wilson, Scott. *Steering through Chaos: Mapping a Clear Direction for Your Church in the Midst of Transition and Change*. Grand Rapids, MI: Zondervan, 2010.

Wood, George O. *Core Values: Serving Christ's Cause with Effectiveness and Excellence*. Springfield, MO: Gospel Publishing House, 2007.

Wright, Christopher J. H. *The Mission of God: Unlocking the Bible's Grand Narrative*. Downers Grove, IL: InterVarsity Press, 2006.

# About Joseph S. Girdler, D.Min

Superintendent, Kentucky
Assemblies of God (USA)

## Education

University of Kentucky, 1984
BA, Psychology
BA, Communications

Asbury Theological Seminary, 1991
MA, Missions & Evangelism

Evangel University / Assemblies of God Theological
Seminary, 2018
D.Min

## Married

Pastor Joe married Renee (Dr. Renee Vannucci Girdler) on
June 7, 1986. Renee is the daughter of Assemblies of God
pastors from eastern Kentucky. Both parents were 100%
Italian, with grandparents on both sides of her family
migrating to the United States from Italy in the 1930s.

Having served as chief resident in Family Medicine and graduating from the University of Kentucky Medical School with honors, Renee is a board-certified family medicine physician with Norton Healthcare Systems in Louisville. She is the former clinic director and vice chair of the Department of Family Medicine at the University of Louisville, as well as the former director of Clinical Affairs and vice chair of the Department of Family Medicine at the University of Kentucky. Her specialties include Women's Health Care and Diabetes, while having further interactions, as well, with International Medicine.

With an extensive background in ministry, she was previously honored by the former general superintendent of the Assemblies of God, Rev. Thomas Trask, and former AG World Missions director, John Bueno, by her selection as the first female in Assemblies of God history appointed to the World Missions Board of the Assemblies of God. She was honored by former general superintendent, Dr. George O. Wood, in receiving the General Superintendent's Medal of Honor, the Fellowship's highest honor for lay individuals in the Assemblies of God (received at General Council 2011, Phoenix, Arizona). Renee was a longtime member of the Board of Directors for Central Bible College and Evangel University. Renee's medical and missions travels/ministries have included Ecuador, Peru, Argentina, France, Spain, Mexico, South Africa, and Belgium.

## Personal

Born: Corbin, Kentucky, June 7, 1962
High School: Laurel County High School, London,
Kentucky. President of Beta Club, 2-year inductee to the
Kentucky All-State Concert and Symphonic Bands
    College: Graduate of the University of Kentucky, 1980–
1984; 4-year Music Scholarship recipient (trpt), President
UK Band, Vice-President Psi Chi, Mortar Board
    Married: Dr. Renee V. Girdler, 1986
    Children: Steven Joseph Girdler, MD, born 1991 (wife,
Julia). Steven is a physician at Mt. Sinai Medical Center,
New York, NY, Orthopedic Surgery.
    Children: Rachel Renee Girdler, MSW, born 1995. Rachel
is a missionary associate to Ecuador.
    Presented "Mayor's Key to the City," Versailles,
Kentucky, 2004.
    Approximately 50 International Mission Trips
    Commissioned Kentucky Colonel, by Kentucky Governor
Martha Layne Collins, 1986.
    Commissioned Kentucky Colonel, by Kentucky Governor
Matt Bevin, 2016.

## Ministry

Superintendent: Kentucky Assemblies of God, 2004–
Present
    General Presbyter: Assemblies of God USA, 2004–

## Present

General Council Assemblies of God USA, Commission on Chaplaincy, (2019–2020)

General Council Assemblies of God USA, Commission on Ethnicity, (2014–present)

General Council Assemblies of God USA, Commission on Evangelism, (2005–2006)

District Missions Director: Kentucky Assemblies of God, 1997–2005

Ordained: Assemblies of God, Kentucky District Council, 1994

Senior/Lead Pastor: King's Way Assembly of God, Versailles, Kentucky, 1992–2004

Associate Pastor, Music, Youth: King's Way Assembly of God, Versailles, Kentucky, 1988–1992

Chi-Alpha College Campus Associates: Morehead State University, Morehead, Kentucky, 1987–1988

## Publications

Girdler, Joseph S. "Royal Rangers Leaders You Are Appreciated," *High Adventure: The Official Magazine of Royal Rangers* (Summer 2006).

Girdler, Joseph S., ed., *75th Anniversary: Kentucky District Council Assemblies of God—2009.* (Crestwood, KY: Kentucky Assemblies of God, 2009).

Girdler, Joseph S. *A Christian's Pilgrimage: Israel.* *http://www.blurb.com/b/6869906-a-christian-s-*

*pilgrimage-israel*. Blurb Publishing, 2016.

Girdler, Joseph S. "The Superintendent Leader-Shift from Pastoral to Apostolic Function: Awareness and Training in Leadership Development for District Superintendents in the Assemblies of God USA." D.Min diss., Evangel University, Assemblies of God Theological Seminary, Springfield, MO, 2018.

Girdler, Joseph S. *Redemptive Missiology in Pneumatic Context*. Crestwood KY: Meadow Stream Publishing, 2019.

Girdler, Joseph S. *Setting the Atmosphere for the Day of Worship*. Crestwood, KY: Meadow Stream Publishing, 2019.

Being raised Southern Baptist and Missionary Baptist, and then attending a primarily Methodist seminary, "Pastor Joe" began ministry serving the college campus of Morehead State University in Morehead, KY, with the Assemblies of God. Followed by four years of music ministry and youth ministry, he was propelled to a lead pastorate in 1992. His welcoming relationships with pastors of multiple fellowships and denominations have served him well in developing a broad and ecumenical approach to church networks globally. Early in ministry he was asked to serve in statewide denominational leadership. Serving initially as the Kentucky Assemblies of God World Missions director for 7 years while simultaneously pastoring King's Way Assembly in the Lexington, KY, area for a total of 16 years, Pastor Joe was then elected as the Kentucky Assemblies of God district superintendent in 2004.

Initially a revitalization project, his pastorate with the King's Way congregation found the church overcoming paramount obstacles from the outset, but then underwent three building programs and grew to an average attendance of 400+ people. A key element was that the church grew their missional stewardship from about $15,000 to an annual missions giving of over $430,000 in only 12 years. The last year of his pastorate (2003) the church attained more than $1,000 per person, per capita missions giving, over and above the church's regular tithes and offerings. The church was honored, of well over 12,000 Assemblies of God USA congregations at that time, to achieve Top 100 status in Assemblies of God World Missions giving. Their ministry site by that time of almost 40 acres and assets of approximately $4 to $5 million at the time of his transition had become one of the strongest congregations in the Kentucky Assemblies of God, baptizing new converts during the morning worship service nearly every Sunday. The church's academic childcare ministry (King's Way Academy) was at the time one of the largest in the region with over 150 children five days per week and a full-time staff of over 25 leaders.

Drs. Joseph and Renee Girdler both serve (present and previous) on numerous boards and committees throughout the Assemblies of God fellowship. Their unique journey of together integrating both ministry and medicine has offered numerous opportunities to encourage next-generational leadership in the callings of God. Of many global travels, his missions ministries have included Argentina, Peru, Ecuador (20+ times), Mexico, El Salvador, Brazil, Italy, Germany, Austria, Spain, France, Belgium, England, Turkey, Bulgaria, and more.

**Contact Information:**
Email: jsgirdler@kyag.org
Office: +1 (502) 241-7111
Website: www.kyag.org
P.O. Box 98
Crestwood, KY 40014, USA

54757945R00126

Made in the USA
Columbia, SC
05 April 2019